Dating With Anxious Attachment

A Guide and Workbook for Those Who Have an Anxious-Preoccupied Attachment Style and Want to Heal Fears of Abandonment and Rejection, Opening Doors to Confidence and Feeling Loved

The Growth Tutorial

Copyright © 2024 by The Growth Tutorial

All rights reserved. No part of this book may be reproduced, stored in a retrieval system, or transmitted in any form or by any means, electronic, recording, mechanical, photocopying, or otherwise, without the prior written permission of the publisher, except for brief quotations used in reviews.

Published by The Growth Tutorial.

The pages in this book are intended for personal use. Commercial use is strictly prohibited without written permission of the publisher.

Disclaimer: This book is not a substitute for professional therapy or counseling. This book is intended solely for informational and self-help purposes. The author and publisher are not responsible for any actions or decisions made based on the content of this book. Readers are advised to seek professional advice for individual situations. By reading this book, you acknowledge that is does not establish a therapeutic relationship, and the author and publisher disclaim any liability for the use or interpretation of information herein.

Table of Contents

Introduction

Welcome to *Dating with Anxious Attachment*. In this book, we will cover topics including what anxious attachment is and where it comes from, identifying the partner you want and the one that you're drawn to because of your attachment, common traits and behaviors of those anxiously attached specifically when it comes to dating, challenges during the dating stage for the anxious, why boundaries, needs, communication, and interdependence are so important to relationships, tools and strategies for overcoming what your attachment style tells you to do and becoming a more secure version of yourself, and thriving in your dating life and the relationship to yourself.

Dating with this attachment style can be frightening, as one tends to believe their partner will suddenly get tired of them and leave, or that their partner doesn't really love them. With this attachment style, it is easy to feel like a burden and always second guess everything, wondering when a sudden change will occur, and planning for the worst *just to be safe*. There are reasons all these harmful things are felt, and ways to challenge them, so you can go from dating with fear to experiencing joy without these negative thoughts.

Keep in mind, when dating, there will be plenty of times *anyone* will have dates that don't work out or relationships that end. These things happen, and it just means you try again to find the person you mesh well with, finding mutual love and understanding. It might feel familiar to blame yourself for breakups or overthinking dates, but as you'll find out, there are reasons for these hurtful thoughts, too, and ways to give yourself the benefit of the doubt, realizing responsibility, but letting go of unnecessary suffering.

First, we will look into the anxious style, then we'll dive into common instances during the dating stage for those anxiously attached, including tools, and then we will do some exercises focused on healing specific hardships for this style.

This is a great step forward for you.

Brief History of Attachment Theory

Developed in the 1950s by John Bowlby and expanded upon later by Mary Ainsworth, Attachment Theory explores the bonds formed between child and caregiver. During the Strange Situation Experiment, young children were left in a room once their mother left, and then a stranger would come into the room, but then the mother would return. An attachment style could be determined by watching how the child behaved during the departure of the mother, the time spent alone with the stranger, and the return of the mother.

A secure style was determined when the mother returned and the child was comforted and soon was ready to play. An anxious style was determined when the mother returned but the child could not be consoled and clung to the mother. An avoidant style was determined when the mother returned but the child ignored her. A disorganized (or fearful avoidant) style was determined when the mother returned, but there was inconsistent behavior from the child like showing fear, freezing, approaching the mother, but then running away.

Breakdown of the Four Attachment Styles

The **secure** attachment style is aptly named since it is the only secure style in attachment theory. Those with this style are confident in their caregiver's ability and responsiveness. They feel comfortable to go out and explore the world, trusting that their caregiver will be there when they return. They know when they need support and comfort that their caregiver will provide that for them. This results in a more positive mindset, growing trusting and loving connections with others and themselves.

This is why in the experiment, the securely attached child calms as soon as the mother returns. The caregiver is a place of comfort and the child sees no reason to feel burdened any more.

Securely attached individuals feel seen, understood, and valued from a young age. During early stages of life, they also felt safe and as though they could comfortably ask for reassurance and validation without any form of punishment. As they grow up, they are able to find a balance between relying on others as well as meeting their own needs. This allows them to feel comfortable showing vulnerability while being interdependent. Most of the time, those with a secure attachment style have it because of the way they were brought up and the relationship they had with their early caregivers and environment. In other cases, the secure attachment style is learned after having an insecure attachment style.

Securely attached individuals tend to have a positive outlook on themselves and others, leading to confidence, openness, and a better sense of peace. They do have negative experiences, just as anyone has, however, they are able to assess the situation in real time, being able to separate people from certain actions.

The other three attachment styles are all referred to as insecure attachment styles due to their inclusion of anxiety and avoidance around self, others, or both, deviating from security.

The **anxious** attachment style has also been called anxious preoccupied, resistant, and anxious ambivalent. People with this style feel intense anxiety in relationships (platonic and romantic). They tend to become preoccupied with the availability of those they are attached to, leading to high levels of emotion, constantly fearing abandonment. They can be seen as clingy, and have difficulty with rejection and self-esteem.

During the experiment, the anxiously attached child would not stop crying because of the immense fear and uncertainty felt by the mother leaving. Anxiously attached individuals may have had caregivers that, though could be very warm, were inconsistent; for example, loving caregivers, but they worked late or traveled often for business. The caregivers could be attentive sometimes, but were seemingly detached at other times. Some caregivers may have been overwhelmed or even unintentionally made the child feel responsible for the caregiver's feelings. Even if there isn't *real* abandonment, perceived abandonment can have the same effect. The mixed signals leave the child confused and unable to know what type of response will be given by the caregiver(s) in the future. This leads to the child interpreting that their needs may or may not get met. In some cases, caregivers may appear overbearing in a way to get their own needs met from their child, many times not even realizing this. At times, this type of parenting may be a result of caregivers being raised a similar way and having anxious attachment themselves.

Those with this attachment style crave intimacy with the constant fear that it will leave when they do find it. Being alone heightens this fear. Since they have low self-worth and a high opinion of others, they tend to gain acceptance through others, feeling the need for outward approval. When they are in a close relationship, they constantly seek to be closer, fearing that any change or distance will result in being abandoned. This can come off as clingy to those close to the anxious individual, and will most times have an opposite effect than desired, pushing others away. It is a continuous cycle for the anxiously attached, feeling safe for a short period of time, and then fearing abandonment again just as soon. It is a rollercoaster of emotions with the highs feeling grandiose and the lows feeling unbearable.

The **dismissive avoidant** attachment style is also known as the avoidant style. Those with this style tend to appear emotionally distant and highly independent. They suppress their needs and emotions and are not usually very vulnerable. When it comes to finding a partner, a dismissive avoidant may have difficulty opening up, feeling it is safer to avoid strong emotions and spend plenty of time alone. They can end up feeling overwhelmed by relationships and self-sabotage when there is a sense of commitment due to fear of intimacy.

In the experiment, the dismissive avoidant child becomes closed off to the mother, feeling as though their needs will not get met even if they try to convey them, and feeling safer if they avoid rather than express their feelings. Growing up, the dismissive avoidant may have had a caregiver that was neglectful or emotionally distant, leaving the child to basically fend for himself or herself. This could even be seen with a loving caregiver who tells their child that it is weak to cry, creating this belief that it is not okay to show emotion. The caregiver(s) may have expected independence from their child or rejected the child when expressing emotions, not meeting the child's needs. This teaches the child to be completely self-reliant, leaving the child with the sense that others cannot be relied on. The dismissive avoidant will place autonomy above emotional intimacy and connection, viewing any type of vulnerability as unsafe since they did not feel safe going to their caregiver with openness.

They appear extremely confident, but underneath is a sense that they are unworthy of love. Whether hiding it or being unaware, there is a hidden fear of abandonment, believing that when someone sees them for who they think they are, they will be left, and so this attachment style tends to leave teetering relationships first so they will not feel that pain of abandonment. They also tend shut down instead of partaking in conflict as this feels too vulnerable for them.

The **disorganized** attachment style is also known as the anxious-avoidant, disoriented, or fearful avoidant style. This style can be seen as a mix between the anxious style and the dismissive avoidant style. You can think of a spectrum with one of these two styles on either side. Someone who is disorganized may show more signs of being dismissive, or more signs of being anxiously attached. This can even change depending on who they are around. If someone who has the disorganized attachment style is involved with someone who is a dismissive avoidant, they may sway more anxious. Whereas if the same person is involved with someone who is an anxious-preoccupied, more signs of their dismissive side will most likely be triggered. They can be hot and cold toward those in their life and be untrusting of their partners, experiencing jealousy due to fearing betrayal.

In childhood, the disorganized individual may have had some sort of trauma early on. This could be neglect, abuse, or some reason to fear their caregiver. Or there may have been other types of trauma where they felt their safety was at risk – early divorce, loss of a parent. Other causes leading to this style could be if something of heavy weight happened that broke the child's trust, if the caregiver became emotionally needy, threatening language was used often, or the caregiver also had this attachment. Inconsistent parenting shows up here, too. They perceive their caregiver(s) as unpredictable, unsure if they can feel safe in their environment and feel comforted by the caregiver since sometimes they do and other times they do not.

They have a positive association with love as well as a negative association with love.

The disorganized individual craves closeness like the anxious, yet fears it as the dismissive does. They tend to have a negative outlook on themselves as well as others. There is a strong desire to become close, but once they do, there are conflicting emotions, making them want to distance, while at the same time, wanting more closeness. This is because, though they deeply want that intimacy, they have a hard time trusting people and fear vulnerability. Believing they'll end up being rejected, disorganized individuals have a cycle of their own, searching for connection, and then becoming afraid of the closeness and self-sabotaging. What makes them feel safe is also what they fear.

Understanding Anxious Attachment

By understanding your attachment style, specifically anxious attachment in this case, you can better become aware of negative thought patterns and actions that can affect relationships. This and other tools will enable you to communicate effectively, manage insecurities, cultivate a healthy relationship with yourself as well as your partner, and address core wounds that have been programmed into you. Without awareness, it is likely the unhealthy patterns will continue in your relationships, even the one to yourself, and you will not be able to recognize it because these thoughts within you driving these harmful patterns are what feel familiar to you.

Holding onto these negative patterns, especially while unaware of what they are or where they come from and why, lead to many dangers in a relationship. These are not your fault, but they are your responsibility to fix. Fears of abandonment, rejection, and not being liked, along with neediness, seeking constant reassurance and validation externally can lead to conflict within relationships and pain within yourself. Of course, it can be healthy to request reassurance from your partner, it is dangerous when their assurance means everything to you, while your own means nothing. These ongoing conflicts can cause individuals to inadvertently sabotage relationships and cause cycles of insecurity to continue.

In terms of triggers, those anxiously attached have their own set of rules for how to cope, but many of these behaviors can be harmful. Reacting poorly to triggers and continuing unhealthy ways of coping can create destructive patterns, lead to misunderstandings, conflicts, and emotional distress, as well as hinder personal growth. But these are done because at some point, this is how you learned to get your needs met. So, when we talk more about this topic, we will find healthier strategies to witness the emotions and fears around these triggers and meet these needs.

In Dating Specifically

Those with an anxious attachment will respond to dating with both fear and excitement for different reasons than another attachment style might.

In childhood, it is likely the anxious individual had positive associations with love, but at the same time, whether perceived or in actuality, love kept being taken away. So, they felt this love, but they also were fearing the next time it would vanish. This caused them to feel the need to cling to love any chance it appeared, and to intensely seek it when it wasn't there. Because of this, during dating, and beyond, they have heightened sensitivity to real or perceived threats of abandonment. They also struggle with self-worth, not thinking highly of themselves to give it to themselves, but believing they require it from outside sources, typically those they've formed an attachment bond with. In childhood, the attachment figures are parents or those raising the child. These attachment figures can change when the same individual becomes an adult, forming these attachment bonds with their partner, or even close friends.

Since they have a low sense of worth, they will constantly seek reassurance and validation from the person they are dating. You can think of this need for reassurance as a cup. When the cup is full, things feel great for the anxiously attached, but when the cup is empty, things feel off and unsafe. The anxious individual does not feel worthy enough to fill their own cup, so by getting reassurance from their partner, the cup fills. However, when something goes wrong or there's an argument, or the anxious has negative thoughts about the relationship, the cup leaks. Then they need the partner to fill it again. If there was a balance between giving their own reassurance and at times asking their partner for reassurance, the cup wouldn't become empty, leaving the anxious with less emotional turmoil, and the partner feeling less overwhelmed. We will cover how to do this and more later on.

Those anxiously attached tend to think in terms of catastrophizing. They think the worst-case scenario, believing this will keep them safer. While it is good to plan and be prepared, always expecting the worst creates more anxiety, and can harm relationships. Anxious individuals view expecting the worst as a way to be ready to deal with it better when the time comes – notice the word *when*. They believe abandonment is inevitable; that no matter how good things are now, they will be left at some point. They also think that catastrophizing will soften the pain *when* someone leaves. If they're ready for it, it won't come as such a surprise. However, this is a painful way to live and to view life and relationships, as well as intensifying and continuing the cycle of believing they are unworthy and unlovable. By thinking this way, they are training their brain to believe that these negative thoughts are the truth. This leaks into, not only relationships and how they view themselves, but also careers, how they take care of themselves physically, and their view of life in general.

Overthinking and overanalyzing is another behavior those with anxious attachment use. They become infatuated with their partner, feeling safe and happy that they aren't alone – something that frightens them. But they still believe one day their partner will become bored with them or stop loving them. In order to be *ready*, they overanalyze their partners intentions, behaviors, and words, creating more anxiety.

This may be happening in the mind of the anxious individual during the beginning of the dating stage, but it usually isn't shown until later. In the beginning, the anxious style is likely excited and hopeful, providing warmth and care to their partner. This will go on for some time before coping mechanisms come into play. But once a sudden change has been felt or they sense abandonment or rejection, they will become triggered. And only knowing an intense fear has arisen, and not knowing how to make it go away, they will react with what they know.

The anxious style may become clingy or needy, fearing their partner will leave them. They seek connection, reassurance, validation, and depend on their partner for emotional well-being. They can become codependent on their partner and people please to get their partner to stay. They struggle to balance closeness with independence, and in conflict they may become distressed, give their partner ultimatums, manipulate, or plead in order to regain connection and reassurance. These things are not done to be difficult or to hurt the other person, but rather, while activated, the anxious individual is looking for the quickest way to feel secure in the relationship and keep abandonment from happening.

Some topics or words discussed might sound confusing now, but we will unpack all of this as we move on. We will also discover tools to use and exercises to promote healthy ways of coping and to move toward a more secure version.

Remember, dating is a two-way street. It is not up to you to "fix" your partner, or to become secure for the sole purpose of fixing a relationship single-handedly. Both parties are responsible and must put in the work.

Congratulations on putting in the work for your healing journey that will show in all areas of your life and your connections.

Strengths of Anxious Attachment in Dating

Having an anxious attachment style has many challenges, and of course this style should be healed, moving toward security. It is also important to be aware of traits that come with it that can be used in a brighter light once secure.

Hypersensitivity: Although being intensely aware of the emotions of others around them is what anxiously attached individuals learned to keep safe, being highly attuned to emotions can deepen emotional connection, which is a good thing if it doesn't become enmeshment.

Expressiveness: Anxiously attached individuals express themselves more than an avoidant would. Sometimes these expressions can feel out of control because the subconscious is trying to figure out how to quickly get needs met, but after learning how to communicate in a healthy way, the openness can go a long way.

Commitment: Anxiously attached individuals are very committed to their partners and want to offer support, energy, and time continually, ready to work through any challenges and keep the relationship. Much of this can come from the fear of abandonment, rejection, or being alone, but when a healthy balance is found between the relationship with the partner and a relationship to self, that importance of commitment can be beautiful for a healthy relationship.

Affection: Warmth often radiates from those with an anxious style. They are able to create a loving and nurturing environment for their relationships. The danger is when the other person becomes overwhelmed and the anxious individual ignores their own needs. Once secure, this balanced affection can be a positive quality for a relationship, especially when the anxious individual gives this same warmth to himself or herself as well.

Emotional Depth: Emotions are continually felt by anxious individuals. They overanalyze and overthink, are constantly worried about people leaving, and have a poor outlook on themselves. Once they begin to question their negative stories and have healthier relationships to self and to others, the emotional depth they're used to can become positive and nourish an emotional connection.

Consideration: Those with an anxious style are constantly looking for ways to make their partners happy or meet their partner's needs. They want to prove they care about them, and also want them to stick around. Doing so, though acting with loving gestures, can sometimes come on too strong for others, and typically, those with this style forget about themselves, people pleasing, rather than finding a healthy balance. However, once a healthy balance is found, and consideration is given to both the anxious individual and the other person, this thoughtfulness can play a big role in nurturing a relationship.

Empathetic: Anxiously attached individuals are wonderful listeners. They provide a safe environment for others to share their thoughts and feelings, and typically are good at keeping things confidential when needed. They rarely show judgement, and they do their best to really listen. However, this style has difficulty knowing where one person ends and the other begins, wanting to take on the problems of others even if it means ignoring their own needs and responsibilities. Going out of one's way for another person can be a loving act; it's when it's constant or so much that someone loses their own sense of self that it gets very unhealthy. Finding balance with interdependence, being able to listen and offer support while not falling into the trap of codependency is where this empathetic nature shines.

Flexibility: Anxiously attached individuals generally go with the flow. They adjust their behaviors and expectations to accommodate their partner or friends, even if it produces resentment or hides their true self. When the anxious becomes more secure, feeling safe to express their true self, and learning to compromise, considering all parties involved, including themselves, this flexibility can be a critical factor in finding fair solutions for conflict, providing mutuality, and help with understanding and other sorts of compromise.

Appreciation: It is common for those with an anxious style to continually show appreciation to others for big and small things, whether spending time with them, getting them a small gift, or remembering a little thing they once mentioned. This style tends to feel unimportant and puts others on pedestals, so if they are made to feel wanted by others, they put a high level of importance on it (and yes, these things are great, but unfortunately, it's that the anxious individual believes they don't deserve it). Once self-esteem and self-compassion are learned, the anxious individual can still be appreciative, but also know they are no less than another person. This expression of gratitude can go a long way, especially with those who struggle to show vulnerability, as the encouragement and appreciation can help them to feel more comfortable opening up.

Supportive: The anxious style is great at providing motivation and encouragement for others, giving time and energy toward the aspirations they know are important to others. They are wonderful at cheering others on and offering assistance to help others reach their goals. However, they rarely give this to their own goals, and rarely praise their own achievements. Once they learn to heal their wounds, they can give this same support to themselves as they do with others.

Pitfall: Core Wounds

Formed from early childhood, core wounds are harmful ideas an individual believes about their very identity. These wounds are deeply emotional and come from suppressed and internalized pain around events or situations. These wounds are carried from childhood, or traumatic events, into adulthood as a means of protection. For example, let's say you have a wound around abandonment because you were left at an early age – your subconscious will remember the negative emotions it brought and the sense of being unsafe, so your subconscious will do its best to watch out for something like that happening again, and perhaps you will cling and people please to make sure there's less chance of being abandoned again and keeping a feeling of safety. These core wounds are held within us, but they are dangerous as they influence us negatively, making us feel poorly about ourselves, and making us think others see us in that same poor light. Once aware of your specific core wounds, since they were programmed into you, you can reprogram them, challenging the negative beliefs around them.

The following is a list of core wounds:

I am abandoned	I am alone	I am unsafe
I am unimportant	I am weak	I am unloved
I am misunderstood	I am stupid	I am unworthy
I am disrespected	I am rejected	I am bad
I am not enough	I am excluded	I am defective
I am powerless	I am helpless	I am unseen
I am disconnected	I am unwanted	I am unheard
I don't belong	I am disliked	I am betrayed
I am trapped		

The next portion is a list of core wounds most typical of the anxious-preoccupied style. Keep in mind, core wounds will vary for different individuals, even ones with the same attachment style, although it is likely most anxiously attached individuals will have the abandonment core wound, for instance.

Before we explore the most common core wounds for the anxious style, let's talk about why it's important to identify and understand your specific core wounds.

The core wounds you have, as we've mentioned before, influence how you view yourself. They also influence how you see the world, and your perspective on people and their behaviors. The core wounds an individual has likely have been carried for such a long time that those negative beliefs feel like the absolute truth – if someone constantly thinks they will be disliked, that thought becomes automatic, and then they'll believe others have that same thought about them, so when they aren't texted back or someone becomes busy and can't hang out, the reasoning given is that they aren't liked, even though that's a story proposed by the familiar negative belief. And then, that same person may cope in unhealthy ways like constantly calling or claiming that person doesn't care about them, all because the assumption based on that core belief that feels like truth. Like with any of the core wounds, after experiencing trauma around this wound, your subconscious is constantly expecting this to happen again, meaning you're constantly fearing the cause of this wound in order to be prepared for it, which as we've mentioned, creates a continuous negative story.

It may seem clear that core wounds can bring on stress, greater anxiety, and depression. Now, take into consideration a dating experience. If a date has to cancel due to an emergency, an anxiously attached individual might personalize that and tell stories that their date is no longer interested. Depending how close the relationship is at this point, the anxious individual might give up, thinking they are unwanted, or they might protest by clinging. Either way, you can see how this would be overwhelming for the date dealing with an emergency, as well as creating unnecessary suffering for the anxious individual. If this relationship had developed connection between these two individuals, the anxious may become preoccupied and in a state of constant stress until the date reschedules or shares some sort of reassurance. And in many cases, the anxious individual might realize they're reacting strongly and not want to, but still do, because they don't know the root of the intense anxiety. In these cases, the anxious individual may genuinely subconsciously be experiencing a fight for survival, believing that if this person leaves, they will be alone and in danger. And something like clinging, is the quickest way they can think to regain that closeness that feels lost.

This is a lot of information right away, but we will get a deeper look into each aspect as we move on. The important thing to know here about core wounds, is the impact they can have on relationships – the one to yourself, and the ones with those around you, including, as we're discussing more closely in this book, with someone you're dating. Becoming aware of your core wounds, learning about them, and using intentional effort and tools to reprogram them will have a positive impact on not only your self-esteem and anxiety, but your relationship to yourself and others as a whole.

Some Core Wounds Most Typical of the Anxious Style:

Remember, there may be more you relate to, or even some that are different than these listed below. Whether you relate to few or most, it's okay. You have the ability to reprogram all of them using tools we will explore further along.

I am abandoned/I am alone: This can come from real or perceived abandonment. It becomes a cycle that is repeated within the subconscious, accepting abandonment as inevitable, expecting everyone to leave eventually. This can cause people to stay in unhealthy relationships, overlook red flags, overcompensate, need constant reassurance, and not set boundaries in fear it will push others away. Those with this core wound can also have a tendency to abandon themselves by ignoring their own needs, not respecting their own boundaries, and never spending quality time alone.

I am rejected: This wound can result from needs going unmet, caregiver being absent, having a traumatic experience with not being chosen in some way. Those with this wound can compare themselves to others and have feelings of jealousy and loneliness. They tend to miss out on opportunities, because they fear that putting themselves out there will ultimately lead to rejection, which comes with many feelings of shame or guilt, as well as heightened negative thoughts. Always expecting rejection makes it hard for someone to show their true self and enjoy life genuinely. For instance, the anxiously attached might over-give or pretend to be different from their true self or never say how they really feel because the rejection hurts more than pretending.

I am unloved: Being given conditional love or experiencing real or perceived abandonment can activate this wound of feeling as though one is unable to be loved. Someone with this wound might believe they have to earn love or that no one will ever love them. Let's say someone is entering the dating stage with someone, but they have this wound. They will constantly feel like they have to do extra just to be loved, or they might always have intense negative emotions believing the relationship can never be equal if they think they can't be loved. Which also is unfair, to not only that person with the wound, but also the person they're dating that really does love them.

I am excluded: This wound can stem from being in a high competition family, being bullied, or having trouble fitting in. Having had experiences like this that stick with the individual, it becomes natural to believe they'll always be left out and think in terms of catastrophe – expecting the worst, believing it's safer to in order not to be taken off guard. But this can increase a fear of rejection, self-doubt, and feelings of emptiness. It causes extreme pressure on one's self and creates feelings of distrust. It becomes automatic to believe one is being excluded because they're disliked, offering negative stories, only deepening pain that has a source that probably isn't accurate.

I am bad: If someone has been told, "*You* are bad," instead of perhaps, "That *action* was bad," at a young age, they may grow up believing they are undeserving because they're bad at their core. People with this wound tend to over-apologize, participate in self-punishment, and try controlling how others see them, fearing if they are seen as *bad*, they won't be wanted. This causes intense stress to be perfect, intense guilt, and extreme sadness when one's standards aren't constantly met.

I am unimportant: This wound means feeling as though one doesn't matter or measure up, typically due to having overbearing caregivers, unmet needs, or getting punished but rarely rewarded. This can keep individuals with this wound from speaking up, feeling as though their opinion doesn't matter. It can cause low self-esteem while having a higher view of others, creating stress as one sacrifices their own needs and only focuses on others. This can cause an intense rift in a relationship.

I am unsafe: This can go hand in hand with fear of abandonment, as abandonment itself feels unsafe. This wound can also come from growing up in an unsafe environment or needs going unmet. Anxious styles may find it difficult to self-soothe as they focused on only soothing through their caregiver and never on their own, not having a healthy balance. So, for instance, as our attachment figures move from our caregiver to usually a partner, think about this in terms of dating. If you soothe through your partner, but are unaware how to soothe yourself, or feel unable to since you haven't had practice, then times your partner is unavailable, or if there's a breakup, you will feel unsafe and go into a state of panic.

I am not enough: This can come from an overly strict caregiver or being put down constantly or always being blamed. It can mean not being good, pretty, smart, funny enough. This wound can deepen other wounds, like rejection, abandonment, disconnection, helplessness, being unwanted, and more. If someone feels as though they aren't enough, they'll start everything believing they don't come close to measuring up and that everyone else is better than them. This creates jealousy, self-doubt, and a painful perspective. When someone with this wound goes on a date, there's an anxious environment from the start.

A Tool for Core Wounds:

Look through the list, including the full list at the beginning of this section. Feel free to circle or highlight the wounds that you feel you relate to, or the ones that you feel jeopardize your dating life the most. There is a place to write them down in the exercise section if you'd rather do that.

Next time you feel a trauma response taking place, try witnessing it. Sometimes, especially in the beginning, you might miss it and react with your normal coping mechanism. It's going to happen, but you can get better and better at recognizing these instances and controlling them instead of them controlling you. When this happens, try remembering how you felt during the trauma response and what caused it.

After you've recognized you're being triggered, name the core wound you're feeling, and there may be more than one. Being aware is *huge*! It's like being able to see your opponent instead of them being invisible. If it's difficult to identify which core wounds you're experiencing, witness your thoughts around your trauma – are you afraid of being left, or not loved, or that you won't fit in?

Once you've realized which core wound(s) you feel, you can better challenge it. Feel it, then question it (do I know I'm purposefully being excluded?, Am I really unsafe?, etc.), then practice soothing yourself to promote more trust in yourself rather than feeling the need to always find safety externally. Again, self-soothing is another topic we will discuss more in depth later on.

Now that you've realized you've had a trauma response, you know which core wound(s) you're experiencing, and you've questioned it, what is your go-to strategy? Be honest.

When you've labeled your coping strategy, think about what need(s) it's meeting. And then find a better, healthier way to get those needs met.

To break it down with an example:

Realize there has been a trauma response. ⇨ Nathan wants to move in with Rebecca, but Rebecca isn't ready for that step.

If helpful, what thoughts show up? ⇨ Nathan may think, "Rebecca is going to leave. I'm not enough for her. She would hate to live with me. She must not really love me."

Identify the core wounds. ⇨ I am abandoned. I am not enough. I am rejected. I am unloved.

What are the strategies usually used (more likely to be unhealthy strategies as the subconscious goes for the most familiar and quickest ways to create a sense of safety; ways that have likely worked before)? ⇨ Nathan talks poorly to himself. He questions Rebecca's love for him. He threatens to leave in an attempt to test her feelings for him. He asks her to reconsider.

What needs are these unhealthy strategies attempting to get met? (Skip to the section on needs if it helps). ⇨ Connection. Reassurance. Being heard. Security.

How can these needs be met in a healthier way? ⇨ Kinder self-talk. Questioning negative stories. Healthy communication. Mutually fair compromise. (These will all be discussed later on as well).

If you'd like to do two worksheets specifically for core wounds, go to page 95 & 96.

Pitfall: Triggers

A trigger can be something that activates a trauma response, reminding us of a moment in time in which we felt unsafe. Certain emotions are activated and this can cause us to use a coping mechanism or protest behavior which we believe will make us return to a feeling of safety. Triggers, being connected to past experiences, will influence how a person reacts to the world around them. When triggered, a person will likely activate or deactivate. Deactivating strategies can be things like stonewalling or withdrawing. Instead of expressing emotions, the user of deactivating strategies downplays anxiety, repressing their feelings in an attempt to feel safe. Activating strategies, on the other hand, can be things like continuously trying to contact someone who won't answer, displaying intense emotions, outwardly seeking a need like validation. The anxious style uses activating strategies as protest behaviors. These strategies are meant to keep one safe and protect against threats, but much like the deactivating strategies, they can perpetuate the situation.

There are also other responses related to triggers, which are fight, flight, freeze, and fawn. Fight shows up as a visible action like shouting or showing anger. Flight is associated with the feeling of wanting to escape or distance in panic. Freezing can be shutting down or trying to act as if you don't exist to not be seen. Fawning tends to betray yourself in order to avoid confrontation, which can be people pleasing or agreeing to something you don't want to.

We will take a look at some common triggers for the anxious attachment style, then in the next section, some common coping mechanisms/protest behaviors, and in the section following that, look at the triggers and protest behaviors again matched up with possible scenarios within dating, and exploring how a secure style might react in the same situation.

Let's make a note here that it is not wrong to be triggered by these things, though it is important to be aware and recognize what is happening internally when you are triggered. It's crucial to investigate within yourself whether you are experiencing a real threat or creating a negative story. Also, be sure to be intentional about how you react. Ask yourself whether your way of coping is healthy or unhealthy. Many times, healthy communication can solve or clear things like this up, that could otherwise unnecessarily snowball into something more, creating more pain and causing more stress to relationships. We will discuss more about coping mechanisms and communication shortly.

Please, also be aware, some relationships just aren't healthy. In these scenarios, we are assuming that these individuals are doing the best they can. In any relationship, it has to be a two-way commitment, meaning that fixing your own attachment issues doesn't promise a healthy relationship. Both parties have to be intentionally making an effort and come together with mutual understanding. It's important to try, but not to attempt carrying the whole relationship and getting hurt because the other person isn't trying.

Common Triggers for the Anxious Attachment Style:

Abandonment: Stemming from inconsistent caregiving or real or perceived abandonment, the anxious style believes that everyone will eventually leave. Even instances of distance or uncertainty that may appear minor can signal to an anxious individual that abandonment is near. When triggered, the anxious individual may seek reassurance and connection to feel safe.

Rejection: Another instance where heightened sensitivity comes into play is the trigger of rejection. Anxious individuals are subconsciously on the look out for rejection, even if it's perceived. They are used to feeling a fear around not being accepted or not being loved for their genuine self. This can be considered an umbrella trigger for several other triggers on this list like canceling plans last minute, not responding to texts, being excluded. Rejection can also take the form of someone needing space or a partner not prioritizing physical affection as much. When triggered, the anxious individual may seek validation and reassurance.

Someone seeming distant while hanging out: This can cause an anxious individual to believe abandonment and rejection are around the corner because they may interpret the lack of presence as a sign of disinterest or as feelings being lost. When triggered, the anxious individual may seek closeness, reassurance, and attention.

Thinking of past negative experiences: Anxious individuals overanalyze and ruminate often; they also keep negative memories stored as a protection mechanism, believing if they are prepared, they won't be as hurt as before. These memories can carry an increase in suffering because they typically are unresolved. By these negative memories being rehearsed over and over, feelings of distrust and unworthiness can become amplified, causing damage to current relationships. When triggered, the anxious individual may seek reassurance and certainty.

Call or text going unanswered or someone taking longer than usual to respond: Anxieties can become heightened when there is no response or an unusual delay in response. Anxious individuals gain a safe feeling of connection when they have constant contact with their partner, and knowing their partner is available for them when they need. In a case like this, the anxious individual might think of the worst-case scenario like an accident or upcoming abandonment. When triggered, the anxious individual may seek contact for a sense of safety.

Being ignored: Whether over the phone or face to face, anxious individuals feel intense feelings of being unsafe. They can interpret being ignored as disinterest, not being enough, and as a threat to the relationship. On the surface, they are being ignored, but underneath, there is a fear of abandonment, a fear of rejection, uncertainty, lack of connection, confusion, anxiety, and unavailability. When triggered, the anxious individual may seek reassurance, connection, certainty, and comfort.

Separation: In the context of an agreed separation, one without threat to the relationship, like a trip where only one partner goes, or going to different schools, or traveling for work, the anxious individual can still perceive this as a type of abandonment. The anxious individual has difficulty self-soothing and forming an internal emotional connection even though it comes easy toward others. Separation for the anxious individual can cause distress and loneliness as they don't typically have a relationship to the self and may go into a panic as fears arise if some sort of connection isn't kept. When triggered, the anxious individual may seek closeness, reassurance, and certainty.

Exclusion: This can mean not being a part of a conversation or not being invited to an event. Whether real or perceived, this will create fears of being unimportant, unwanted, possible abandonment, and rejection. When triggered, the anxious individual may seek inclusion, attention, and validation.

Lack of reciprocity: Anxious individuals love to give to others. They are typically warm people, wanting to make others happy, though it is also important to know, especially awareness as the anxious, that overcompensating and over-giving can be a means to people please or to keep people around thinking one isn't good enough to be wanted otherwise (which is where self-esteem comes into play, which we will explore later). Where lack of reciprocity becomes a trigger is within the context of resentment. Anxious individuals will cross their boundaries and give all their time and energy, but then when the same isn't done for them, they may perceive it as being taken advantage of or being unappreciated. When triggered, the anxious individual may seek appreciation and acknowledgement.

Disagreements/Arguments: Anxious individuals feel safest when there is no conflict or disagreements. They may believe having an argument is a road to abandonment, which is why it's usually the anxious individual volunteering to take the blame and make amends, because otherwise, they fear they will be left alone. The anxious style views disagreements as threats to relationships, heightening their anxiety and making them question the stability of their relationship. When triggered, the anxious individual may seek to resolve the conflict as quickly as possible, connection, reassurance, and peace.

Distance: Anxious individuals feel unsafe when there is physical or emotional distance and will do whatever they can to close that gap and reconnect. They have difficulty self-soothing and will fear abandonment from the distance. When triggered, the anxious individual may seek connection and reassurance.

Last minute canceled plans: Typically, the anxious individual will grow very excited for plans with a partner. If plans are canceled, the anxious individual may wonder if their partner really cares or if they should be worried about being replaced. They may believe their partner doesn't find them to be enough or that a lack of interest has resulted. When triggered, the anxious individual may seek reassurance, attention, and closeness.

Uncertainty about the future being expressed: From a partner not being ready to label a relationship to not being sure when they want to solidify a commitment, an anxious individual may personalize the uncertainty, believing that the hesitation in moving forward is about them. When triggered, the anxious individual may seek reassurance and certainty.

Spending more time with others: The anxious individual may see this as being excluded or put on the back burner, or as a personal attack to their importance and worth. This doesn't have to mean someone getting more time from a partner in general, but even if an anxious individual is used to a certain amount of time, and then that changes to less time, the anxious may see that as a threat, fearing abandonment and rejection. When triggered, the anxious individual may seek certainty, connection, attention, and consistency.

Secrets: This can be the anxious hearing rumors about their partner that they were unaware of, their partner setting their phone down facedown, or that their partner has been having struggles but didn't share that information with them. This can make the anxious feel as though they are not important enough to know certain things or create worry about distrust. When triggered, the anxious individual may seek transparency and communication.

Pitfall: Protest Behaviors

As we will be discussing protest behaviors, these are the reactions caused by triggers. Note, a protest behavior is a coping mechanism. These behaviors are used because they have worked in the past for protection. Unhealthy protest behaviors typically have short-term benefits, but long-term or delayed costs. However, when triggered, the short-term benefit looks the most attractive, especially when awareness is unaccounted for.

Craving connection with others and fearing being alone, protest behaviors for anxiously attached individuals are likely to create closeness and harmony, usually achieving these things in the quickest way possible.

During triggers, anxiously attached individuals use activating strategies – things that involve action, like a fight response, for instance. They express themselves or actively try to achieve safety by things like continuous calling or creating jealousy. These strategies ultimately get needs met. Constantly calling, though an unhealthy protest behavior, meets the need for connection. Without awareness of better and healthier ways to get these needs met, it's likely these unhealthy patterns will continue being used, which will cause more stress to both the anxious individual and the partner.

Anxious individuals will sometimes even tell themselves not to send another text after having just sent five back-to-back, but they probably still will. This is because the conscious cannot outwill the subconscious. The subconscious is responsible for the majority of our thoughts, it holds our emotions and memories and beliefs, and its influence can overpower our conscious intentions. Which is why if you want to deeply reprogram a pattern in yourself, you have to start with the subconscious. Where the conscious uses language, the subconscious uses imagery and emotions.

A Tool for Subconscious Reprograming:

For an example, let's say you react in fear of being abandoned, even though you know you're safe, your subconscious is picking up signs that you might be in danger of abandonment, so you constantly call your partner, causing a rift within the relationship.

If you want heal your wound around abandonment, you can't just tell yourself you're okay and won't be abandoned, because that's not speaking to your subconscious where this belief is coming from.

So, you'll have to use imagery and emotion. This is where you'll find memories, which will also ignite emotions, challenging negative beliefs.

You can start by saying the opposite of "I'll be abandoned," which will be, "I am connected" or "I can be connected." It's important to keep away from phrases like, "I'm not abandoned" because your mind will still think about being abandoned, much like climbing a ladder and telling yourself, "Don't look down," which causes you to think about the danger in falling rather than getting to the top.

Once you find that positive opposite, remember times you felt connected. Take yourself back to that memory and feel the emotions you experienced. Or, imagine being connected and try feeling those emotions you might feel. These instances can be small moments; you don't have to remember anything grandiose. The important part is that you feel the emotion of whatever it is you're trying to reach.

Try doing this with several memories, and try doing it each day. The repetition is important because these beliefs and fears were made from repetition over time, which is why to reprogram these negative beliefs into something positive, you'll need to repeat the process so the positive will become automatic rather than the negative.

If you'd like to do a worksheet specifically for subconscious reprograming, go to page 96.

Some Common Protest Behaviors for the Anxious Attachment Style:

Keep in mind, the reasoning for why these protest behaviors are used in each explanation is not to excuse them, but to create an awareness which will lead to an easier transition into healthy strategies.

Constantly contacting: This serves as a way to regain connection. This can mean calling or texting continuously, showing up unexpectedly to meet someone, or checking social media to view someone's activity. The anxious individual has likely been triggered by a fear of abandonment, rejection, or some sort of distance, and they believe that by making contact, they will gain closeness and certainty and things can be okay where they would currently feel unsafe.

Catastrophizing: When things feel wrong, the anxious may think of the worst-case scenario in an attempt to get ahead of the issue or to not be caught off guard. It makes them feel as though they have some sort of control in this frightening situation whether it is a real or perceived threat.

Overanalyzing: Being highly attuned, the anxious individual is able to spot more cues than the average person. Being attentive to the actions and emotions of others has kept them safe, but sometimes they can overly monitor people, causing them to guess motives which can sometimes be correct, and other times incorrect. Since those with an anxious style have a poor view of themselves, they are more likely to interpret negative emotions or actions as a personal threat rather than possibly someone having a bad day or being tired.

<u>Excessive apologizing</u>: If the relationship appears to be in jeopardy, the anxiously attached will apologize whether they believe they should or not. During an argument, the anxious, having low self-esteem and low self-worth may believe that if they don't do everything they can to smooth things over, they will be abandoned. However, always taking the blame can cause resentment, becoming an issue later.

<u>People pleasing:</u> This can come in the form of saying yes when you want to say no, or vice versa. In a sense, it is crossing and disrespecting your own boundaries, or not setting them in the first place. It can be by giving time, money, effort, or other things you aren't able or don't feel comfortable to give. The anxious will prioritize the other person's needs above their own in an attempt to secure connection and approval, afraid that if they leave the other person disappointed, they will be rejected and abandoned.

<u>Over giving:</u> This can also create resentment as it opens the door to an imbalance in the relationship with a lack of reciprocity. However, this is an unhealthy tactic the anxious individual uses to combat the fear of abandonment. They don't believe they have enough to offer in who they are, so they feel they need to give everything they can in order for people to stay around. They fear that if they don't give more than they're comfortable with they won't be wanted any more. By doing so, anxious individuals perpetuate a poor view of themselves, and ignore their needs and boundaries, abandoning themselves as they fear others will do.

<u>Seeking reassurance:</u> Anxious individuals don't think highly of themselves enough to accept their own reassurance, so they are constantly seeking it externally. Being unaware of how to give themselves reassurance, their supply of it runs low, which causes fear, and pushes them to receive it from someone else so

they can feel safe again. Gaining reassurance gives anxious individuals a temporary relief.

Threatening to leave: The anxious may voice empty threats about leaving the relationship. The anxious probably doesn't want the relationship to end, but wants to know the other person would be afraid to lose them. They aren't sure how to express these heightened emotions and only realize they feel neglected in some way. A threat of this magnitude serves to capture the attention of the other person. They use this protest behavior in an attempt to regain connection and receive the reassurance they crave.

Testing: Coming from their desire for approval and assessing the strength of their relationships, anxious individuals will check to see how much someone cares by creating an environment or situation for them to prove the extent of their love. This can come in the form of asking something they already know the answer to that is supposed to relay an amount of admiration, or by setting things up to prompt a response from another person in hopes it will show the anxious what they want to see.

Creating jealousy: By flirting with someone else so their partner sees, the anxious may hope that their partner will react with jealousy, *proving* they are cared about. If the partner does react with jealousy, the anxious individual will feel important, loved, and wanted.

Possessiveness: Having both low self-esteem and a fear of abandonment, the anxious can become possessive of a partner, fearing that if they don't have control, their partner will find someone better or forget about them. There can also be a fear behind not having their partner around since the anxious can feel lost while on their own, not having a deepened sense of identity as they typically find their identity in someone else. By keeping a partner close, they feel safer.

Criticizing: This is done in an attempt to get heard and a way to express the pain they feel, but it tends to backfire as these unhealthy coping mechanisms all do in the long run. Being unaware of how to communicate in a productive way, the anxious individual will likely tell the other person what they did wrong and how they did it, which causes the other person to feel criticized and possibly want to retreat, thinking more about how to defend himself or herself and less about what the anxious is saying, though the anxious is trying to close the rift between them and the other person in hopes the other person will do *better* so the relationship will last.

Guilt tripping: The anxious can manipulate to get their needs met. This can be done intentionally or unintentionally, as in most cases it is not done maliciously, but likely out of fear, which does not excuse it, but hopefully brings more understanding.

Scenarios & What a Secure Style Would Do Instead:

Scenario for abandonment: After on-and-off dating for ten months, Sarah, an anxious attachment, and Rick have broken up again. This triggers Sarah as she tells herself stories about how she wasn't good enough and won't ever find anyone to stay, and she constantly tries regaining contact with Rick, texting him every day, which increases her anxiety when she gets no reply.

What a secure individual might do in this scenario: If Sarah had a secure attachment, she could try communicating in a healthy and direct way with Rick about their relationship downfalls and work on them separately or together, depending what those issues are and what they feel comfortable with. However, if there is no genuine compromise, a secure person could learn from the relationship, understand some things don't always work out but it doesn't mean everyone leaves, and nurture a relationship to self.

Scenario for rejection: Alex, an anxious attachment, and Lois had been dating for two months when Lois tells Alex she needs space. Alex takes this personally as rejection. He fears that maybe he did something wrong and that the relationship is in jeopardy. Believing he will be left if he allows Lois the space she's asked for, he clings to her. He tries giving her more space, but his fears win out and his neediness triggers Lois, causing more problems in the relationship.

What a secure individual might do in this scenario: If Alex had a secure attachment, he might understand that Lois's need for space may not have anything to do with him, but rather herself. He would remember that everyone has their own perspective and their own needs, and Lois may feel more comfortable having time to herself sometimes. Alex may ask for reassurance in a direct and healthy way, letting Lois know he respects her need for space, but if she could reassure him that the relationship is going well it could provide relief.

Scenario for someone seeming distant while hanging out: Paul, an anxious attachment, and Lily have been spending time together at Lily's house for the past two hours. Paul was hoping to chat or cuddle up and watch a movie, however Lily has been scrolling on her phone, and whenever Paul starts a conversation, Lily doesn't engage. This causes Paul to overanalyze the situation. He determines that Lily must have lost interest in him because usually she seems happy to see him. Paul figures whatever she's looking at on her phone must be more important than spending time with him and he quickly becomes saddened.

What a secure individual might do in this scenario: If Paul had a secure attachment, he could question his stories around Lily's disconnectedness. Instead of coming to the conclusion that Lily has lost feelings for him, he could remember all the times she's been happy to see him recently, proving to himself that just because she's not fully present right now doesn't mean she's tired of him. He could gently bring up that he's noticed her preoccupation and ask if everything is okay, to which she might let him know she's had a rough day at work, calming Paul's possible anxieties and allowing room for him to comfort her even if that means giving space, instead of trying to defend against an unconfirmed threat to the relationship.

Scenario for thinking of past negative experiences: Daniel, an anxious attachment, and Kellie have been dating for a month. The dates have been going well and both seem to be having a wonderful time together. But Daniel begins having doubts. Things have been so great, he's waiting for the relationship to go sour. He begins catastrophizing after thinking of his negative experiences with dating. He remembers being cheated on and lied to. He remembers another relationship where everything seemed to be going well until he and his last partner started bickering which led to them breaking up. He's afraid the same will happen with Kellie, and now when he thinks of the new relationship, he fears for the time things will go wrong.

What a secure individual might do in this scenario: If Daniel had a secure attachment, he would look at the peaceful first month as a good sign. He would know that all relationships are bound to have arguments, but healthy relationships can work out solutions. He might remember negative dating experiences, but know those don't define his current relationship, and if anything, he can take positive feedback from them.

Scenario for a call or text going unanswered or someone taking longer than usual to respond: Renee, an anxious attachment, and Phil have been dating for a year. The relationship has been going fairly well, having its ups and downs. But today, after three hours, Phil hasn't responded to Renee's text. She knows he's at work, but usually he's pretty quick to respond, so Renee becomes worried. Her fears become intense as she wonders if Phil has been in an accident or if she did something to make him not want to talk to her. She texts him a couple more times, then calls him. She thinks if she could just get some reassurance that he and the relationship are okay, she'll feel safe again and her anxieties will subside.

What a secure individual might do in this scenario: If Renee had a secure attachment, knowing Phil was at work, she might assume he's busy or stuck in a meeting. Of course, if he didn't arrive home at his usual time, she might become worried for his safety. But his current lack of availability wouldn't bother her. She would be patient, taking part in her own job or a hobby, allowing Phil to reply when he became able.

Scenario for being ignored: Grant, an anxious attachment, and Sue had a small falling out a day ago. Ever since, Grant has been stressed, wondering what will happen between the two of them. He fears Sue will leave him, and even if they do mend things, the current distress from her being upset with him is causing heightened anxiety. Grant doesn't know what's going on since he can't get a response from Sue. What if she's leaving him? What if she finds someone to replace him? What if this changes how she feels about him? Grant picks up his phone and starts apologizing, taking all the blame, doing whatever he can think of to fix things.

What a secure individual might do in this scenario: If Grant had a secure attachment, he may be stressed from the small falling out he experienced with Sue, and he may send a message to communicate that he wants to find a solution. If Sue still ignores him, he can understand that she may need more time to process her feelings and reestablish an internal safe environment. After a little time has passed, they could figure out the solution together. Now, if Sue kept ignoring him for an ongoing amount of time or was doing it to be malicious, Grant may question the healthiness of the relationship and make a decision from there.

Scenario for separation: Abby, an anxious attachment, has her anxieties grow after her boyfriend, Clyde, leaves for a work trip. He'll be gone for two weeks. At first, Abby misses him, but feels okay. But then she becomes fearful, wondering if he misses her, if he'll enjoy time away from her, if things will change when he gets back. She feels alone and has difficulty with her emotions. She feels bored and depressed, feeling disconnected from herself, and not really knowing what she wants or needs.

What a secure individual might do in this scenario: If Abby had a secure attachment, she would of course miss Clyde, and stay in contact with him. It could be hard to be away from him for those weeks, but she would focus on her hobbies and work and friends. She would be aware of her needs and work through her emotions by self-soothing, not needing Clyde to fulfill her identity.

Scenario for exclusion: Jack, an anxious attachment, and Pam have been dating for a few months. They both enjoy each other's company. Jack loves spending time with Pam because she fulfills needs he's unaware of like adventure and novelty. He says that she makes him feel whole and he doesn't know what he'd do without her. This weekend, Pam went out with her friends to get some much-needed girl time. Jack saw her out on social media and became saddened that he didn't get an invite since she usually invites him everywhere. He wonders why she didn't want to see him and wonders if she still loves him. So, he goes out to the same place with a few of his friends, and not long after they arrive, Pam spots someone flirting with Jack. Jack doesn't engage, but he hopes it makes Pam jealous so he can have confirmation that she does still care about him.

What a secure individual might do in this scenario: If Jack had a secure attachment, he would question any stories he had around feeling excluded. He would remind himself that Pam usually invites him to things, so she does like being around him, and their relationship has been going well. Jack would also take into consideration that Pam enjoys her time with her friends, and just because he wasn't invited that time, it doesn't lessen his importance to her.

Scenario for lack of reciprocity: Dylan, an anxious attachment, has been feeling taken advantage of by his partner, Sam. Anytime Sam needs something, Dylan drops whatever he's doing and goes to help. He even buys her dinner every time they go out and does his best to remember any events that are special to her. With Dylan's birthday coming up, he mentions that a certain basketball game would be so fun to go to, hoping that Sam takes the hint and gets them tickets to go, figuring if she remembers, she cares, but if she doesn't, she either must not be listening to him or doesn't care. He's also started becoming resentful.

What a secure individual might do in this scenario: If Dylan had a secure attachment, he would become aware of his boundaries and set them, then he would respect them, making sure no one crossed them, including himself. If Sam asked for help and it wasn't an emergency, Dylan would help if he could, but not if he was unable. If buying dinner each time became uncomfortable for Dylan, he would let Sam know in a healthy manner that he wouldn't be able to get the check every time, or he may even suggest they eat in more often or ask if she would be able to get the next meal if she felt comfortable with that. Instead of expecting Sam to *know* he wanted basketball tickets for his birthday, he could directly tell her that if she was looking for something to get him and was able to, that he would enjoy going to a basketball game with her. Anxious styles pick up on subtle cues much better and can expect others to do the same, but other styles don't typically have the same hypervigilance as the anxious or disorganized.

Scenario for disagreements and arguments: Julie, an anxious attachment, and Bill are having an argument. Bill wants to use the afternoon to go fishing, but Julie wants them to do something together. Julie becomes anxious, afraid that if Bill doesn't get his way, he won't love her anymore. To make the relationship feel safe and diminish the perceived threat of it ending, Julie people pleases, agreeing that Bill should go fishing, and builds resentment.

What a secure individual might do in this scenario: If Julie had a secure attachment, she would understand that a healthy relationship won't end over an argument, and that every relationship will have disagreements. It's how they are handled that matter. She knows Bill isn't her enemy and that she isn't

Bill's enemy. They're a team working against the problem for a solution that is mutually fair. She also knows she doesn't have to earn love, and having an argument doesn't change each other's feelings. Julie may realize there's a compromise available, which leads Bill to take Julie fishing with him, so Julie gets to do something with Bill and Bill gets to fish.

Scenario for distance: Erin, an anxious attachment, becomes worried when Frank distances himself. They had been spending so much time together during the first four months of dating, but suddenly, Frank seems too busy with his work to make much time for Erin. Seeing Frank's distance as a threat to the relationship and personalizing it, Erin decides to threaten to leave, catching Frank off guard and damaging the relationship even though it's Erin's intention to save it from the perceived threat by having Frank worry about her leaving and them regaining closeness.

What a secure individual might do in this scenario: If Erin had a secure attachment, after noticing Frank's sudden distance, she may communicate in a healthy way, letting him know she's not attacking him or his need for space, but that she's wondering what it means about their relationship. Frank may reply that he didn't even realize he'd been so distant and that he felt he was losing himself in the relationship and needed to remember to focus on his work, too. They could both come to a compromise that allows for Frank to continue giving time to his work while still making time for Erin.

Scenario for last minute canceled plans: Gary, an anxious attachment, and Brenda had plans to go to a movie. Gary showed to pick Brenda up, but she wouldn't answer the door. After calling, Brenda rushed to the door, but wasn't ready to go. By the time she got ready, the movie would have started. She apologized, telling Gary she was looking after her niece and nephew today and they wore her out. She took a nap, but was asleep for longer than she had meant. Gary takes the situation personally, believing that their date must not have meant enough to Brenda. He criticizes her, telling her she must not love him and wondering how she could sleep through something they planned a week ago. Both become stressed and regretful that night.

What a secure individual might do in this scenario: If Gary had a secure attachment, when hearing that Brenda had overslept, he wouldn't personalize it or create unnecessary suffering internally. Especially if Brenda made it clear the movie date with him had been important to her, Gary would understand mistakes happen. Instead of letting his emotions control him, Gary may ask Brenda if she'd want to watch a movie in instead.

Scenario for uncertainty about the future being expressed: Harry, an anxious attachment, wonders about Maggie's commitment when she expresses a desire to date for two years before getting married. Over the past year, Harry has fallen for Maggie, and he thought she had too, but now he has doubts. He wonders why he ever thought he was good enough for her and believes she doesn't actually want to be with him. He starts becoming controlling, hoping that keeping her closer to him will keep her from catching feelings for someone else.

What a secure individual might do in this scenario: If Harry had a secure attachment, he would understand that just because Maggie wants to wait another year before thinking about marriage, doesn't mean she thinks any less of him. He, too, will understand that marriage is a big commitment and want to make sure they are making the right decision as they continue to learn and grow together. Harry won't become possessive of Maggie because, being secure, he has a good relationship with trust and confidence.

Scenario for secrets: Naomi, an anxious attachment, watches Kyle set his phone on the counter facedown. This raises question for Naomi. She figures he must be trying to hide something, and wonders what it is. When he leaves the room, she checks his phone, but there's nothing out of the ordinary.

What a secure individual might do in this scenario: If Naomi had a secure attachment, she may not think twice about the phone being set facedown on the counter. There's been no supporting evidence for Kyle to be up to anything hurtful, and they've been able to trust each other. If it does end up bothering Naomi, she may communicate with Kyle, asking if there's a reason he sets his phone facedown, and sharing that she could use some reassurance, but unless there have been real trust issues between the two of them, Kyle's phone being facedown would most likely not bother Naomi.

Important to Learn: Needs

The way people meet or ignore their needs is a large factor in determining how someone lives life and the experience they have. Each person has different needs, which will have an effect on how we behave, what we desire, and how we can perceive others and the world around us. When it comes to what are known as the Six Human Needs, each person will rank these differently, but they are all important, and when one is left out, there is an imbalance felt.

Tony Robbins's model of the Six Human Needs is as follows:

Certainty: The need for safety, security, protection, comfort, stability, and predictability.

Uncertainty: The need for change, excitement, novelty, freedom, and exploration.

Significance: The need to feel important, needed, to matter and have meaning, have some sort of positive status.

Love and Connection: The need for mutual love, closeness, to connect with someone.

Growth: The need to grow, learn, develop, strive for something important.

Contribution: The need to give, help, provide service to others.

There are many other needs such as love, freedom, communication, clarity, certainty, uncertainty, affection, harmony, order, belonging, trust, support, cooperation, contribution, growth, meaning, joy, power, integrity, authenticity, effectiveness, play, touch, security, learning, rest, honesty, celebration, purpose, efficiency, dignity, intimacy, consideration, mutuality, spontaneity, compassion, understanding, autonomy, acceptance, wholeness, peace, ease, interconnection, creativity, self-expression, appreciation, inspiration, hope, reassurance, choice, nurturing, health, movement, relaxation, companionship, respect, listening, empathy, exercise, privacy, to be seen and heard, friendship, community, space, consistency, challenge, skill, novelty, adventure, presence, simplicity, focus, accomplishment, confidence, discovery, warmth, caring, kindness, humor, beauty, structure, independence, gentleness, spirituality, bonding, pleasure, protection, sense of self, sharing, inclusion, responsibility, partnership, equality, significance.

Some Common Needs for Anxious Attachment:

Reassurance, communication, emotional availability, physical contact, validation, inclusion, commitment, predictability, encouragement, loyalty, caring, support, emotional intimacy, acknowledgement, recognition, affection, openness, quality time, comfort, trust, honesty, understanding, reliability, being understood, security, cooperation, consistency, mutuality, bonding, certainty, love, connection, partnership, appreciation, being seen, being heard.

When our needs are not met and we aren't aware of what our needs are, we can feel emotional pain because these are things, as the word suggests, that we *need*.

Growing up, anxiously attached individuals may have had their needs met sometimes, but others times those same needs may have gone unmet because of the inconsistency. During childhood, an anxiously attached individual may have been used to meeting the needs of their caregiver that they ignored their own, or a caregiver didn't leave *any* room for a child to learn how to meet some needs, or a caregiver may have been too concerned with their own needs that they neglected the needs of their child, or perhaps there were multiple children in the house, so some got their needs met, while others didn't.

Those with an anxious style are very good at meeting the needs of other people. If an anxious individual is dating someone with a need for being heard, the anxious individual will likely drop everything to listen to this person. As the anxious style puts their partner on a pedestal, meeting their partner's needs not only feels safe for *proving their worth*, but also, seems worthwhile since the anxious individual views their partner with importance, while view their own self with low value.

Those anxiously attached struggle with needs because many times, they are:
-   Unaware of their own needs
-   Are not internally present so have a difficult time learning their needs
-   Ignore their needs because they have low self-esteem
-   Ignore their needs in order to people please
-   Ignore their needs by crossing their boundaries

Anxiously attached individuals will sacrifice their needs continually for their partner. At first, it may make them feel good and safe. By sacrificing their needs for those of their partner, they believe they are making their partner happy and giving their partner a reason to stay. (Of course, you can meet the needs of your partner out of love; it's when those needs are being met out of fear and you're crossing your own boundaries where it becomes a problem.)

After some time of continuously sacrificing to keep the partner's needs met, the anxious individual will become resentful, believe they are being taken advantage of, and are unappreciated. There will be an imbalance in the relationship. The anxious individual may believe their partner is simply selfish and ungrateful. Without awareness, it really will seem like this. (And of course, there are unfortunately times in which people are selfish and ungrateful, but with awareness, you can determine whether that's the case or if resentment due to over-giving is the culprit.) This resentment can cause a rift in the relationship, leading to both parties feeling misunderstood and confused. More problems can grow from this, snowballing into major arguments and breakups without being aware of the root cause.

At times when the anxiously attached individual is alone or single, they may feel a sense of emptiness. While in a relationship, they tend to get their needs met externally through their partner, even without knowing what their needs are. This is because a huge need for the anxious is connection. Being in a relationship allows for connection. They are also drawn to people who deliver their suppressed needs. So, even though they aren't aware of their needs, they are good at finding those who fulfill them. During their relationship, the anxious individual is trying to meet their partner's needs by giving to them what seems to make their partner happy. Without knowing what their own needs are or how to meet them, the anxious individual will feel stuck and often depressed.

Everyone, based on their own unique upbringing, has a perspective that is different from that of others. However, everyone expects everyone else to use that same lens to look at the world. So, since an anxiously attached individual feels good when they have emotional intimacy with their partner, they think the partner must feel the same way. But if their partner is an avoidant, that person may be uncomfortable with much emotional intimacy. However, if neither is able to communicate this in a way the other will understand, it can lead to problems in the relationship.

It works the same way if a partner tells an anxious individual that they need space in the relationship. The anxious will automatically go into a panic because they know that if *they* asked for space in the relationship, it would mean they weren't interested anymore. However, with an avoidant, or even in some cases someone who is secure (though the extent of *space* may be different), their feelings may very well be the same, but they feel the need to give their job or hobbies more attention, too, or simply find they need more time to recharge, with no insult to the anxious.

Becoming aware of your needs is extremely beneficial to a positive mood and feeling good, learning and setting your boundaries, effectively communicating, and promoting a relationship to yourself. When you know your needs, you'll be able to meet them, empowering yourself. And when you're able to express your needs, you'll be able to communicate better, have a better relationship with expectations, and be more understood by your partner.

A Tool for Identifying and Meeting Needs:

We are typically drawn to our needs, and we feel out of balance with ourselves when our needs are not being met even if we don't know where the discomfort is coming from.

Think of things you are naturally drawn to. This can be traits people have or activities you enjoy. Let's say some of your hobbies include skiing and boating. Perhaps you have high needs around adventure and being outdoors. Let's say there's something about Edward you really admire. You can think he's great as a person, but also what qualities about him does he have? If you feel comforted by him and like that he listens and keeps secrets, then perhaps you have needs around comfort, being heard, support, loyalty, connection.

Another way of doing this is thinking about times you've felt poorly. Let's say everyone was talking over you at lunch, which made you feel awful and maybe even angry. What needs weren't being met? In this case, you may find you have high needs around being heard, respect, consideration. Or maybe you've been working on a project on the computer at home for several weeks and feel uncomfortable. With some thought, you may find you have a need around travel and movement and freedom.

And sometimes, just by looking at a list of needs, certain ones can stand out to you.

After you've identified your needs, you can find ways to meet them and express them, instead of relying on external sources.

To meet your needs, think of the needs you've identified. Then, come up with strategies to meet these needs on your own. For instance, if you have a need for comfort, you can snuggle up with a blanket to a movie, or you could draw yourself a warm bath. It can be helpful to write down reasons why meeting your own needs rather than always getting them met externally will become, or is becoming, a strength for you.

We will cover expressing your needs in the section on communication.

If you'd like to do three worksheets specifically for needs, go to pages 89, 90, & 91.

Important to Learn: Boundaries

Boundaries are essentially limits on what we find acceptable or unacceptable which contribute to each individual's well-being. Boundaries can vary from person to person as one individual may be comfortable with something that another individual is not. Respecting our own boundaries and the boundaries of others is extremely important for a secure life.

There are different categories of boundaries, and they are as follows:

Time Boundaries: How much time do you feel comfortable giving?

Intellectual Boundaries: How will you respond to the thoughts of others around your ideas?

Material Boundaries: What objects, or how much money, are you comfortable sharing?

Physical Boundaries: Who and what are you comfortable being around, and how close is appropriate?

Sexual Boundaries: What are you comfortable with sexually?

Emotional Boundaries: What do you feel comfortable communicating, and how much can you take on emotionally from others right now?

Those anxiously attached have difficulty with boundaries as they fear by having them, they will set themselves up to be rejected and abandoned. And since the anxious style doesn't have a good relationship with boundaries, and is unfamiliar with them, by seeing the world through their own lens, it's easy to treat others as if they don't have boundaries, crossing limitations others have put in place.

To put this in perspective, let's say a coworker has someone with anxious attachment to cover their shift. The anxious individual has an important test to study for, but they fear that if they don't cover the shift, this coworker will dislike them, so the anxious individual takes the shift, violating their own boundary, that in this scenario, they may not have even realized they had. Taking it a step further, say the anxiously attached failed their test because they didn't get to study. Now, they most likely will start building resentment up around the coworker, and be upset internally, causing more anxiety. That is an example of disrespecting your *own* boundary.

Now, let's take a look at disrespecting someone else's boundary. We'll use Derrick and Tanya for our example. Derrick has told Tanya he loves spending time with her and would enjoy her company when they've scheduled a time to meet, but that he doesn't feel comfortable when people randomly show up at his house. If Tanya then shows up at his house unannounced, Tanya would be violating *someone else's* boundary – in this case, our character, Derrick.

Boundaries are set in place to protect you. This does not mean that by setting a boundary everyone will automatically know it's there, or if they do know, they may not respect it, because we cannot control others. This is why it is important to express your boundaries (which we will cover in the section on communication) and uphold them. An example of this could be if you've made it clear (by telling someone directly, not by expecting them to know) that you have a boundary for being on time, but your partner is coming to pick you up thirty minutes late for the fourth time in a row. By upholding your boundary, you could set a time, and if your partner doesn't arrive by then, send a text that you'll meet them at the event instead. If your boundary continually gets crossed and there's no effort being shown, it may be time to assess whether the relationship is healthy.

The way boundaries empower us is by giving us the ability to allow or not allow certain behaviors. Remember that we are all human and will make mistakes and be forgetful at times. So, there may be times you will need to remind someone of a boundary, maybe even more than once, and when their effort is shown, acknowledge that.

As stated before, each person can have different boundaries. This means that we cannot base what someone else's boundaries are off the ones we have. For instance, one person may not be bothered by someone calling them first thing in the morning, so they assume it's okay to call their partner at that time. However, their partner doesn't get up as early and has a boundary around their sleep. If partner 2 expresses this, then hopefully partner 1 will respect it. On the other hand, if partner 2 doesn't say that it bothers them and either gets angry each time partner 1 calls, or ignores partners 1's calls, a misunderstanding may be created which could lead to unnecessary conflict in the relationship. This is why it is so important to communicate your boundaries.

When anxiously attached individuals do identify their boundaries and set them, it is difficult then for them to follow through with them. Their fears around their core wounds keep them from speaking up. They would rather deal with the consequences of allowing their boundaries to be crossed rather than face the fear of abandonment, rejection, or being disliked. However, most of the time, especially within healthy relationships, these fears are stories that have been fabricated because of deep-seeded fears carried in the subconscious that are there for protection, but actually have the opposite effect in these cases. This is why it is important to question negative stories when it comes to keeping boundaries.

When boundaries are violated, it can lead to frustration, anger, confusion, hurt feelings, resentment, anxiety, and it can ultimately weaken relationships. And the anxiously attached, being fearful of abandonment, will typically overlook these intrusions as they believe it is safer to do so, all the while bottling up these emotions.

⇨   Identify your boundaries

⇨   Set your boundaries

⇨   Create healthy strategies for keeping and reinforcing your boundaries

⇨   Express your boundaries

⇨   Respect and uphold your boundaries

⇨   If boundary is violated by someone else: remind them of the boundary and how to respect it; use a healthy strategy created for reinforcing boundaries

⇨   Positively acknowledge when someone is actively showing effort to respect your boundary

⇨   If you violate your boundary: ask why you did it or what you feared by keeping it; be gentle with yourself; acknowledge your courage when you do uphold your boundary

Also . . .

⇨   Recognize the boundaries of others & ask when unsure

⇨   Respect the boundaries of others

⇨   When you're tempted to cross the boundaries of others, ask yourself what you fear will happen if you respect them

If you'd like to do three worksheets specifically for boundaries, go to pages 92, 93, & 94.

Important to Learn: Healthy Expectations

An expectation is a belief that someone *should* do something, or that something *should* happen.

Those with an anxious attachment tend to expect a lot from others and get lost in their fears and heightened emotions when their expectations are not met. For example, an anxious style may expect that someone is always available, and when that person is not available, the anxious individual may feel stress and anxiety as well as feeling hurt and let down by that person, because typically when the expectations of the anxious style are not met, it will be taken personally, giving into negative beliefs about being unloved or not good enough.

Anxious individuals most likely carry the belief that they must rely on others to be safe and for their needs to be met. Therefore, their basis for survival is to expect from others, which is why it can feel frightening when expectations are not met, because the anxious individual will feel unsafe.

Anxiously attached individuals can have unrealistic expectations leading to greater likelihood of disappointment. They also place their partners on pedestals, which creates even greater expectations. They may expect a partner to always answer their calls, make them *the* priority, or spend all their free time with them. They may expect that there should be no conflict and that if there is, it's a threat to the relationship.

"Mindreading" is a typical habit of the anxious style. This is when someone expects someone else to know or do something without explicitly telling them. For example, an anxious-preoccupied may mention that they like a pair of shoes, expecting their partner to take the hint that they'd like them for a gift. If the partner doesn't pick up on this, the anxious individual may assume their partner doesn't really care about them. The anxious individual is afraid that if they express what they need or want, they will be rejected. It can also be a test of sorts, believing if a partner does automatically know what they want, the two must have a deep connection which can make the anxiously attached feel safe, connected, and understood.

When the word *should* is used, judgment is already being added. It makes for a tenser and more negative environment internally and externally, actually heightening anxiety. And for the person having something unrealistic or unknown expected of them, they can become confused, irritated, or be triggered to feel as though they're inadequate.

It's important to be aware of your expectations and ask if they're realistic and if you've expressed them directly.

A Tool for Expectations

When you start by questioning your expectations, you're making sure they're fair and realistic. An example of this would be to ask, "Is it fair to expect my partner to come to every event I invite them to?" And when it's realized that this is an unrealistic and unfair expectation that will ultimately create unnecessary stress internally for the anxious and overwhelm the partner, one can create a more realistic expectation, and make sure to express it. This could look like having an expectation that the partner makes an effort to come to important events, but knowing that it won't always be doable; then to express it, one could say something to the effect of, "I understand you won't be able to make all the events, but it would mean a lot to me if you made an effort to come to some that you are able to attend."

It is important to be prepared for compromise as well. Let's say you expect to see your partner five times a week, but your partner expects to see you three times a week. A compromise can be made if it's deemed fair by both parties that you will both do your best to see each other four times a week.

During these times you find yourself expecting or thinking with *should*-language, ask yourself whether it's fair and what you're needing, then identify a healthier way to get that need met rather than only expecting it.

When you catch yourself expecting your partner to read your mind, ask yourself why you don't feel comfortable speaking up to express yourself. What fears do you have in doing so? What need are you getting met if they automatically know what you want?

It's important to remember that someone automatically knowing what you expect or always living up to your expectations isn't realistic and can cause damage to both parties and the relationship as a whole. Healthy relationships are not built on guesswork, but rather on communication and the ability to listen and learn.

If you'd like to do two worksheets specifically for expectations, go to pages 99 & 100.

Important to Learn: Self-Esteem

Self-esteem is how you view yourself and feel about yourself. Those with an anxious attachment style have negative internalized beliefs, like the core wounds discussed earlier. During childhood, inconsistency and needs sometimes being met, while other times going unmet, could have established a wound of being unworthy, as the child is too young to understand it's not their fault their needs are unmet sometimes. Since anxiously attached individuals search externally for love and reassurance, they don't feel good enough to be able to give that to themselves, causing their self-view to suffer. Instances of rejection can also cause poor self-esteem, as well as overanalyzing and creating negative scenarios which outside of the anxious perspective may not have been personal or may have been misunderstood. The anxious style also compares to others, as we've mentioned, by placing partners on pedestals. All that along with previous relationships that may have failed and internalizing that and taking the blame for the breakup, the anxious is constantly bombarded with attacks to their self-esteem, mainly from the stories they've been telling themselves.

When practicing self-compassion and learning more about yourself, identifying your needs, respecting your boundaries, and spending quality time with yourself, your self-esteem will grow. The positive feelings will outweigh and challenge the habitual negative stories.

A Tool for Self-Esteem

Negative stories and negative self-talk are detrimental to self-esteem. Think about how many times a day you speak poorly toward yourself, doubting your potential, questioning your worth and abilities. Recognizing that, and realizing how many days you've been speaking to yourself in those hurtful ways, it is easier to understand why this negative self-view is so powerful. It's been repeated over and over, day in and day out, as a habit. When something goes wrong, maybe the first thing you do is blame yourself, and maybe that comes automatically because it's the go-to when anything does go wrong.

With the above in mind, think what can positively change if you speak better to yourself. Knowing that all that negative self-talk and those negative stories have lessened your self-esteem, think about how your self-esteem can flourish by speaking kinder to yourself. Perhaps how you would speak to a friend or a child.

Think of challenges in your life; things you've been struggling to overcome. Instead of telling yourself you can't or that you aren't good enough, or that you don't know how, identify steps to achieve your goals. Things like, "I haven't yet, but I can learn how." Or you can break down your setbacks into reasons why you haven't overcome them yet, and then question their validity. For example, "I'm too stupid to start my own restaurant. I won't be good enough." You can ask whether these are true, or if these have been negative beliefs stored inside you that you run on autopilot now. Then you can challenge those negative beliefs, questioning the wounds themselves, and creating strategies for how to overcome the obstacles.

Another important tactic is to keep track of how many times you compare yourself to someone else each day. What types of things do you say or believe about yourself when you do this? Does it make you feel good or badly about yourself?

Meeting your own needs, learning to express your needs, setting and reinforcing boundaries, and feeling comfortable in your own space will also heal your self-esteem.

If you'd like to do two worksheets specifically for self-esteem, go to pages 97 & 98.

Important to Learn: Communication

Without healthy communication, there can be misunderstandings and an increased risk for needless conflict. Notice the word, *healthy*. One can believe their way of communication is effective, but healthy communication is different from simply being able to express something.

Let's go over some examples of unhealthy communication:

Criticism: Expressing fault toward the other person will block the chance for a healthy conversation. This tactic will cause the other person to go on the defense, and they won't hear what you're trying to communicate while being prepared to defend.

Defensiveness: Again, if the right words are not chosen to show that you come in peace, the other person will be too preoccupied with defending against your words rather than listening to them.

Stonewalling: Instead of active communication, someone using this tactic may become silent or try leaving the environment as a way to avoid conflict or avoid the emotions that come with it.

Passive-Aggressiveness: This is an indirect way to show one is angry or disappointed without directly expressing it. It can show up as the silent treatment or as insults masked as compliments. It is more likely to spark problems than solve them.

Blaming: By giving blame to the other person, you are creating a me-versus-you situation instead of attacking the actual issue as a team. Each person has a role to play in a conflict.

Manipulation: This can show up as gaslighting, making someone second-guess their reality. It creates doubt of one's own experiences. Guilt-tripping can show up here as well, in which one tries making the other person feel bad as a way to lessen their own blame or get their needs met through that person.

Dismissal: Invalidating the other person's feelings, making them feel undervalued. This can also appear when someone brings up a concern, but the other person is dismissive of it.

Lashing Out: By insulting, making rude comments or sarcasm, or attacking someone with words in other ways, it creates another me-versus-you scenario, making it harder for relief, peace, understanding, and compromise to be found.

Interrupting: Without allowing the other person to finish their thoughts or their side of the story, it makes it difficult or impossible to find understanding. By dominating a conversation, one doesn't just feign control of the situation, but makes it harder to find a mutual solution.

Shouting: Rather than solving a conflict, shouting will likely intensify the problem, escalating emotions. By using intimidation, even if unaware of the level, it diminishes trust and support between two people. Though shouting is used to become heard, it ultimately is an ineffective way for any lasting solution.

Fawning: Used mostly during conflict, one might people please or apologize for the sole reason of *ending* the conflict in order to feel safe. This can also look like letting the other person talk without sharing your own experience out of fear.

Let's take this a step further by looking at a selection from the previous grouping that is most common for the anxious-preoccupied style. The following explanations are for awareness and understanding. It is important to replace unhealthy ways of communicating with healthy ways of communicating. Note, there are more unhealthy ways of communicating than listed, as there will be more healthy ways of communicating than will be listed; and it is possible for an anxious attachment to relate to more or less than what is listed below, however as these are typically the most common, we will highlight this selection.

Criticism: The anxiously attached uses this as a way to point out flaws they see in their partner, hoping that if their partner knows what they're doing *wrong*, they will stop. This is also used by anxious individuals as a way to produce reassurance from their partner.

Passive-Aggressiveness: Since the anxiously attached has fears around speaking up, it feels safer to them to indirectly express themselves. This can come from a fear of confrontation and rejection. They may even fear being abandoned or being seen as bad. However, this is likely to cause more issues and leave the base problem unsolved.

Blaming: Anxiously attached individuals can experience intense guilt, especially since they can become enmeshed with their partner and feel responsible for those around them, even for things they have no control over. By blaming the other person, they are able to alleviate some of that guilt.

Guilt-Tripping: By becoming the victim, anxiously attached individuals may evoke a response in their partner that causes their partner to take care of them rather than engage in confrontation. This can provide reassurance and attention from their partner and alleviate fears of abandonment. However, this can increase guilt in the other person and cause an imbalance in the relationship, as well as delay solutions to conflict.

Fawning: Anxiously attached individuals, as they fear abandonment and rejection, may find it easier in some cases to take the blame and be the one to apologize for everything rather can allow conflict to take place which heightens their anxieties and other fears. By people pleasing, the anxiously attached is able to make their partner happy and maintain a safe feeling of connection. They are used to sacrificing their needs and trying to meet their partner's needs, so doing this within the context of conflict is familiar to them. However, this will lead to resentment, unresolved problems, and an imbalance in the relationship as a whole, as well as less chance to understand each other.

Here is a quick look at some healthy ways of communication:

Respect & Acknowledgment: Even while having a disagreement, it is important to show respect toward the other person, just like you want to be treated. Also be sure to acknowledge and validate the other person's feelings, while being considerate of yours as well.

Directness: Instead of being indirect and fearful, it is important to communicate in direct ways, making sure there is clarity rather than ambiguity.

Transparency: Being open and honest, truly expressing how you feel and what you need is necessary to make sure you are understood. It also helps the other person gain more trust in you.

Empathy & Understanding: Even while in conflict, it is important to show compassion toward the other person and yourself. Just as you may be experiencing negative emotions, so is the other person even if it shows up in different ways for them. Remember their perspective is different from yours, and it is necessary for you both to understand the other's lens.

Assertiveness: Using this to respect yourself, you can also respect others. Assertiveness is not a synonym for *mean* or *rude*. It is taking yourself into consideration and being fair to yourself, while still holding respect for the other person. While being open to compromise (mutual benefits), you can use this to communicate boundaries, preferences, and needs.

Gentleness: It is important to remember what the other person means to you. Conflict doesn't have to mean *fighting*. And arguments don't have to be *bad*. When disagreements arise, you can both use gentleness with each other, speaking calmly.

Teamwork: Remember that conflict should not be a me-versus-you situation. The other person is not the enemy. The enemy is the problem, and the other person is your ally. Though disagreements will arise within conflict, it is important to find understanding and support each other, searching together for a fair solution against the problem.

Problem Solving & Compromise: Like the above, rather than fighting with each other, using unhealthy language, and not listening to one another, try to search for a solution, constructing a healthy compromise.

Active Listening: Both people should be able to share their thoughts and feelings. It is important to note that since we all have our own perspective, one person will have a different experience than the other. Be careful to listen, try to understand, and then respond respectfully, as they should do for you as well. When both parties feel heard, that is where understanding is found, which leads to healthy compromise.

Feedback: This should be given in a constructive manner, rather than with rude criticism. Express feedback toward the behavior rather than the person. Be open to feedback as well.

As we've covered, each individual sees the world, others, and himself or herself through a different lens. This means that if intentions, needs, and other important factors aren't expressed, it's difficult to understand each other.

Anxiously attached individuals are uncomfortable with using healthy communication because they are not used to it. They are typically good at bringing things up – for instance, if they want more connection, they may make sure their partner knows this, however they might not use healthy ways to do this, which tends to have an opposite effect than what they desired.

Those with an anxious style are likely to catastrophize before engaging in communication, thinking of the worst-case scenario, scaring them away from directly communicating. Their lack of self-confidence also undermines attempts at communication since they will talk negatively toward themselves, doubting their capabilities to address concerns or create positive change. When communication does happen, those anxiously attached are more prone to reacting and using activating strategies causing disconnect and possibly thinking less rationally, especially when fears of abandonment and rejection are triggered. And as they rely strongly on others for approval, they are likely to suppress their needs and disrespect their boundaries in order to maintain a sense of safety and keep the other person happy.

A Recipe for Healthy and Direct Communication:

⇨ Come in peace   ⇨ Be prepared to listen

⇨ Express clearly   ⇨ Show respect and gentleness

⇨ Use "I" language   ⇨ Be specific

⇨ Challenge the problem, not the person

When communicating, be sure to:

⇨ Acknowledge the other person peacefully

⇨ Express your feelings, express what you need

⇨ Express how you specifically need it

⇨ Ask for confirmation of understanding

⇨ Be ready to listen and be respectful of the other person

Using the above tools, you can be sure to become heard by the other person, as the other person will not feel attacked by you. Keep in mind, this works for healthy dynamics; sometimes other's will not be open to hearing you, and that's when you need to assess the overall health of the relationship. Now, some people may want to wait to communicate, and by this, it means that some people need more time to process their emotions. For instance, a dismissive avoidant will need more time than an anxious-preoccupied to work through their emotions before feeling comfortable to communicate. Or, some may find certain environments feel safer to communicate. For instance, someone may ask that the conversation wait until you arrive home rather than while at an event.

We all give out of our own needs. Just like we can sometimes forget that others have a difference perspective than we do, it can be difficult to remember that others give as they wish to receive. If someone loves hiking, they might book a cabin in the mountains for a week, thinking it's the best gift ever. And it is thoughtful, because to them it would be special, and they're trying to share that with someone they care about. However, the other person might not like the woods, and would put more importance on a relaxing trip to a beach. The key here is to see the thought behind what is given, and remembering that communicating needs is very important to better understand each other.

To express needs:

Meeting your own needs is important, especially as you regain a relationship to yourself. However, there will be times you need to express your needs to your partner.

Anxiously attached individuals may have fears around expressing needs. It is important to figure out what those fears are for you, whether rejection, becoming a burden, expecting mindreading, or something else. Then you'll want to question your stories around these fears. And then find reasons why it is a good thing to express your needs – you can be understood, your partner will be able to respect your needs better, it can lessen your anxieties.

After you've done that work, prepare to communicate your needs:

⇨ What is your need?
⇨ Why is it important to you?
⇨ How can this need be respected?

The above can look like, "I have a need around certainty. It's important to me because I feel unsafe when there is a sudden change. If there is a change that takes place, can you let me know why, so I don't create negative stories around it?"

As for expressing boundaries, it's important to let someone know when one has been crossed. This can be done both with assertiveness and with gentleness and respect. By letting someone know a boundary has been crossed, you lessen the chance of it happening again.

When you feel discomfort or anger or hurt, there may have been a boundary crossed. When you decide one has been crossed and you're ready to express it (after questioning your fears around expressing it), try this formula:

⇨ What was the boundary? What triggered discomfort?
⇨ Why is this boundary important to you?
⇨ How was your boundary crossed?
⇨ What are the consequences? (If necessary.)

The above can look like, "I have a boundary around being ignored. When I'm ignored, it creates confusion and hurt. When we were arguing the other day and I couldn't reach you, I became more anxious, which was hard for me because I was already anxious due to the argument. I understand if you need some time to process before speaking, but can you please let me know that you need that time? If ignoring in this way continues, I'll need some time to focus on myself and reassess our relationship."

In no way should the consequence be a threat that is meant to test or scare the other person. It should be a healthy consequence that considers yourself if someone continually disregards your boundaries. It is also important to stick to these, which is a way to respect yourself and your boundaries.

Some may think communicating like above gives others *ammunition* to use against you, knowing what hurts you. If anyone behaves in this way, it is an instance in which to assess the health of the relationship. In a healthy relationship, the other person will use this information to create relief, not more stress.

Do note, not all boundaries have to be explained. The most important part is that you know what your boundaries are and you respect them. The above example is to acquire understanding in a relationship. Some boundaries are negotiable, while others are not. For instance, a negotiable boundary may be you expecting to spend time every day with your partner, but your partner needs more time alone to recharge, placing a boundary on having their time alone respected; respecting each other's needs, you can alter both boundaries by having a certain number of days for individual pursuits while keeping in touch via phone if both parties are comfortable with that. A non-negotiable boundary could be for your partner to treat your parents with respect.

Communication Script 1:

The underlined words and phrases are what you will replace for your own experience.

Partner, I'm not criticizing you, and I appreciate that you reschedule canceled plans. When our plans do continue to get canceled, it makes me feel unimportant and disappointed. I feel unimportant and disappointed because I become excited and make sure I'm available for these plans. I needed certainty and transparency. This can be given in the future by making plans when we are sure they will work, though I understand emergencies happen. Does this make sense? Is there anything you'd like to add?

Be sure to get specific about ways in which something can be given, since, for instance, support to one person may look like a hug, while support to another person may look like help running errands.

Communication Script 2:

Partner, I can see you may have felt trapped when I kept calling you yesterday. I felt unloved because I thought you didn't want to talk to me. Can we find compromise together?

Be sure to find compromise – considering both you and your partner. The beginning is very important as well – acknowledging their possible feelings.

How It All Relates to Dating for Anxious Attachment

Those with an anxious attachment style are likely to have social anxiety from a fear of rejection and a fear of being disliked. While telling these stories, it can be hard to trust that someone likes you for you. While going on dates, the anxiously attached may give into core wounds, unaware that their negative thought patterns come from these unresolved wounds. This can cause the anxious to appear preoccupied while on a date, tell hurtful internal stories while on the date, fear that they have to pretend in order to keep their date's attention, and question their worth, overanalyzing anything that could have been perceived as *wrong*. If no second date is offered or agreed to, the anxious may take it personally, believing they weren't good enough, repeating negative stories and lowering their self-esteem. If a second date is offered or agreed to, they may think of it as a favor or as if they did *well enough*, rather than looking at it as mutual benefit. As the dating continues, they'll constantly view any uncertainty or change as a threat, and wonder when abandonment will come. They will view their own failure, real or perceived, as a reason for their partner to break up with them, constantly living in fear and walking on eggshells, their fears taking control.

Core wounds are important to know and heal because otherwise, these will constantly control your thoughts. You may be thinking good thoughts and having a good time on these dates, but if your subconscious keeps sneaking negative thoughts in, trying to protect you but actually doing the opposite in this case, your thoughts are more likely to align with your wounds because these are the stories you're familiar with. If you have a core wound of being excluded and your date wants to go to lunch with *the guys* or *the girls*, you may feel left out and negative thoughts may branch off that core wound. Whereas if you've resolved this core wound or have been working on it, you may not be bothered and be genuinely happy for your partner to spend a lunch with *the guys* or *the girls*. Same scenario, if you felt you weren't spending enough time together, you'd feel comfortable to communicate this, and assuming the relationship is healthy, your partner would hear you and find time to spend with you, compromising somewhere for both of you rather than sacrificing in a way that would cause resentment to build.

Understanding your triggers and coping mechanisms will allow you to realize why you feel certain emotions and give you a chance to pause and find a healthier strategy rather than activating unhealthy familiar ones. For instance, if you're on a date and your date is ten minutes late because traffic was detoured for an accident . . . before knowing the reason, you may internalize it, giving into your core wounds, telling yourself hurtful stories, and then cope in a possibly unhealthy way – maybe calling the date several times or criticizing the date for being late or asking if they *even* plan on showing up. Instead of jumping to conclusions, when a trigger is activated, you can use better tools to question stories and find better ways to cope – as we will explore in the toolkit section.

When you know your needs, you can find ways to meet them yourself or express ones you need help with. In this way, you are allowing for balance, allowing you and your partner to be interdependent, relying on yourselves, but also able to ask for help (assuming your partner is doing this as well). When you are aware of your needs and feel comfortable meeting them, you empower yourself, meaning you won't likely stay in an unhealthy relationship for the reason of not being alone. You won't fear when you're alone because you know you'll be capable of meeting your needs. When you don't feel like you *have* to always have a partner to be safe, you give yourself the opportunity to find someone who is truly a match for you rather than settling.

Once you have healthy expectations and respect both your boundaries and those of others, you're less likely to be triggered needlessly. When you express expectations, it allows you and your partner to be on the same page or find the same page together. You'll be less likely to feel disappointed when you don't need to be. You'll build your self-esteem when you set and keep your boundaries, and you'll feel less resentment. By respecting the boundaries of your partner, you'll be helping to keep the relationship healthy, making your partner feel understood.

When your self-esteem rises, you'll treat yourself better, speak to yourself better, and overall feel better about yourself. When others see this, they'll be likely to treat you better too as we teach others how to treat us. Boosting your self-esteem will help you replace negative thoughts with positive ones, and it will make you desire a good partner rather than any partner. When you care about yourself, you'll want someone who holds the same values you do and who loves you. You won't ignore all the red flags in order to make sure you aren't alone. Self-esteem will help you find a good partner.

Communication is huge in general and for dating. When you know how to communicate, you'll be able to ask important questions as you and your partner get to know each other better. You'll be able to express non-negotiables without fear keeping you quiet. You'll be able to navigate arguments and find compromise. You'll be able to respond better to your partner. And instead of criticism and blaming disguising themselves as communication, you'll know the difference between unhealthy and healthy ways to find solutions.

Anxious Attachment Pairings

In this section, we will explore the anxious attachment style matched with other styles. Of course, there are many possibilities for how these matchings can go. We will look at common ways each style may interact with the anxious in terms of dating.

Anxious & Secure:

As an anxious starts dating a secure, the anxious will feel seen and heard. They'll feel appreciated and accepted, and their fears will likely stay dormant for a while. The anxious will feel comfortable giving to the secure, providing love and warmth and a listening ear, which the secure will appreciate and likely express that thanks. However, as the relationship gets more serious, the anxious may have fears begin to creep in as their hypervigilance may pick up perceived threats, or they may hold onto mistakes the secure has made, interpreting such things as danger. Worried the secure may abandon them and unsure how to express these fears or being afraid to, the anxious will cling. The secure won't react in the same ways other insecure styles would, however the clinginess will likely overwhelm the secure, and not understanding the cause of the clinging, the secure will take time on their own. The anxious may people please to keep the secure partner around, which will grow resentment. At some point, the anxious may become bored with the secure partner as the lack of chaos in the relationship will appear as a lack of passion for the anxious. The anxious grew up with inconsistency and has experienced it through life, feeling familiar with it and unsafe without it. There may be arguments, but the secure partner is likely to approach these conflicts in a calm manner, possibly even promoting a healthier side of the anxious. However, the anxious is not likely to stay after they equate security for boredom, being unaware of the root.

Anxious & Anxious:

An anxious dating an anxious will appear great at first. Both of them will feel connected and understood. They will both be great listeners and make the other feel heard and seen. They will meet each other's needs, ignoring their own, which will later cause resentment. This is because one anxious may have certain needs the other anxious doesn't. For instance, if one anxious has a high need for adventure and spontaneity, this anxious may put together last-minute trips, thinking this is something their partner may want, as we give out of our own needs. The other anxious may have a higher need for predictability. Neither will communicate their reasoning, and neither's needs will be met even though they are both sacrificing. Without expressing their needs or attempting to meet their own needs, their anxieties are likely to grow, as is their resentment.

Anxious & Disorganized:

This pairing will gain a strong connected relationship, viewing their upcoming highs and lows as passion. In the beginning, the two will share and have a bond that may feel unbreakable. Even though the disorganized will feel safe opening up to the anxious, this vulnerability will later cause the disorganized to shut down, fearing that they've allowed too much to be known, afraid that the anxious will see their flaws. The anxious, not understanding the real reason behind the withdrawal or the fears of the disorganized, will take this sudden distance personally. The anxious will believe the disorganized is about to leave them, so the anxious will cling, thinking this will keep the disorganized around. Once this happens, the disorganized will react with their avoidant side by distancing more, or will lash out at the anxious. Neither knows how to use healthy communication, so the disorganized will go into fight or flight mode while the anxious is likely to use fight or fawn. After pushing the anxious away or lashing out, the disorganized will feel guilty and will try reconnecting with the anxious. The anxious, likely going through panic, as we've mentioned earlier, will jump at the opportunity to rekindle the relationship. The anxious may try talking about what happened, and the disorganized may be open to it, but with their avoidant side triggered, they are more likely to shut down. And since the anxious will be more afraid of losing them, the anxious will let it go unresolved.

Anxious & Dismissive Avoidant:

The anxious and avoidant together are known for the anxious-avoidant trap. The anxious will be drawn to the inconsistency as they were in the example with the disorganized. It will feel familiar to them. The intense highs and lows will be confused for passion by both the anxious and the dismissive avoidant. However, in the beginning, this appears as the perfect pairing to both partners. The anxious will find traits they wish they had, and the dismissive avoidant will feel the same way about traits the anxious has. As time goes on, these same traits the other admires will become the traits that trigger them. For instance, the anxious will admire the dismissive avoidant's independence, but will become triggered by the space they need. And the dismissive will admire the warmth and love from the anxious, but will begin to feel overwhelmed by the intensity. The dismissive avoidant will feel cared for and supported, which they didn't feel much in childhood. The dismissive avoidant will also feel heard and seen, which they have core wounds around; and they will feel able to trust the anxious, which is huge for the dismissive avoidant since they grew up believing they couldn't rely on others. They still will not want to rely on the anxious, but they will feel they can trust the anxious. One or the other will become triggered first, which will begin the cycle. It can even be something small. The anxious may feel a slight distance and try getting closer, which will cause the dismissive avoidant to withdraw, or the dismissive avoidant will fear their feelings for the anxious and create space to maintain their sense of self, which will cause the anxious to cling. The anxious has a fear of abandonment and a need for closeness. The dismissive avoidant has a fear of intimacy and a need for freedom. The coping mechanisms either uses actually triggers the other more. Neither knows how to use healthy communication, so this will go on with them both becoming confused, hurt, feeling misunderstood, and disrespected. The anxious may people please to keep the dismissive avoidant around, then become more confused that the dismissive avoidant doesn't do the same, as these two types are the most likely to show love in the most different of ways. And when we don't receive love in the way we give it, we may believe love isn't there. This cycle can cause many breakups and reconciliations. The pushing and pulling will continue until both partners find awareness and learn to heal.

The Five Love Languages

Understanding your love language(s) and that or those of your partner can help you both give and receive love better. Though everyone may enjoy all five of these ways to show love, there usually is a top one or two. Gary Chapman found people give and receive love in different ways, and one person's way to show affection will be different from another. These are ways we show love to everyone in our lives.

Though it can be different for each person, the anxious-preoccupied style is more likely to have words of affirmation, physical touch, and quality time.

It is important to remember that you may feel more loved when you receive a hug from your partner (physical touch), but your partner may feel more loved when you pick a flower to give (gifts). Communicating your love languages can help to understand, love, and support each other better.

Words of Affirmation:

Feeling loved by someone vocalizing what you mean to them. Receiving words of praise and positive remarks. Feeling appreciated and accepted and important when hearing these. Things as seemingly simple as thank you for paying for dinner, that was really thoughtful or you sounded great at your presentation today will go a long way, especially for someone with this as a top love language.

Quality Time:

Feeling loved by spending time with someone. Keep in mind the keyword here – quality. Two people sitting in the same room while one person is on their phone the whole time and the other is doing homework will not feel like this is fulfilled. Quality time is enjoying each other's company, partaking in the same event, talking with one another, playing a game together. Spending two hours of quality time will make someone feel more loved than five hours of distracted time.

Acts of Service:

Feeling loved by someone putting in the effort to help them or doing something kind and thoughtful for them. This can make someone feel like they have a teammate and they have someone who cares about them and thinks about them. Helping them with a project like yardwork, building a shelf, cooking dinner, even accompanying them to run errands. Note here that this is mostly valued when it's offered instead of being asked.

Gifts:

Feeling loved by receiving gifts. This does not mean they want to be showered with jewelry and cars or care about the monetary value of a gift. Here, it really is the thought that counts. They appreciate the time put into picking something out and that they were on your mind. It could be surprising them with the hat they've been wanting, or dropping their favorite lunch off at work, or as small as picking them a flower.

Physical Touch:

Feeling loved by being shown physical affection. This does not have to mean sexually. It can be holding hands, hugging, cuddling, having some sort of physical contact. For those that prioritize this, it can boost emotional connection, helping with trust and vulnerability.

How Anxious Attachment Views Relationships

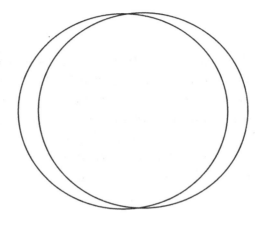

How Secure Attachment Views Relationships

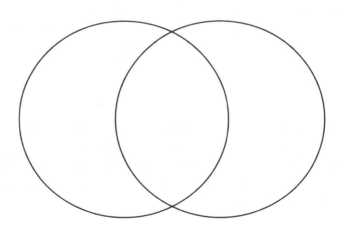

Anxious Attachment & Breakups

Of course it depends on the connection, feeling, and time of the relationship, but for breakups in general, the outcome can feel excruciating for the anxious individual. Unlike the avoidant, those anxiously attached will experience the worst of the pain immediately. They will go through intense emotional distress as their abandonment wound will take hold, making them feel lost and alone. They can experience frightening emotions like sadness, despair, anxiety, and depression.

As anxious styles have a high need for certainty, breakups become scarier as uncertainty is triggered, creating higher anxiety. The anxious will worry about their future, wondering how they'll live without their partner. They will continually ruminate, overanalyzing everything said and done, finding blame within themselves and their ex-partner. They will become obsessed with finding out what went wrong and what, if anything, could have been done to prevent it. These ongoing thoughts will lengthen the pain and make moving on a harder task. Although, moving on to the anxious proposes danger, so they would rather think of ways to mend the relationship. They are searching for familiarity and security.

The anxious will seek some sort of reassurance. They may constantly try contacting their ex via phone or showing up where they think they might be. They may get in contact with their ex's family and friends. Or they may seek comfort from their own friends and family.

As anxious individuals are familiar with telling themselves negative stories, they will continue this trend, talking negatively toward themselves while they need comfort. They provide themselves little comfort and therefore search externally for it. Becoming preoccupied with the breakup, they may have little strength and motivation to do normal tasks. So many of their triggers have been activated at once that daily life becomes survival for them. It may also take an anxious longer to recover as they must find ways to cope during the times they are alone, and build their self-esteem and relationship to self.

While in a relationship, the anxious will lose what little relationship to self they had as they continue to ignore their needs to meet the needs of their partner. When a breakup occurs, they're so familiar with getting their needs met through their partner, and unaware of how to meet their own needs, that their needs go unmet, causing more discomfort and fear.

Between negative self-talk, negative stories, and disrespecting their own boundaries, the anxious has low self-esteem. When a breakup occurs, having low self-esteem makes those negative stories seem more plausible as self-doubt creeps in. And after finding their identity in their partner, when the partner is gone, they feel lost and don't have a sense of who they are or what to do. They may have a need for comfort, connection, reassurance, understanding, support, etc., all needs they are capable to receive internally, but without the awareness of those specific needs or how to receive them internally, they become stuck, looking for external ways to feel okay.

However the relationship ended, their wounds of abandonment, rejection, not being enough, among others will be triggered all at once, and without having a healthy way to manage those fears and pain points, they will cope in familiar ways like ruminating and reaching out to their ex to feel some sort of relief. As they have a high need for connection, when they can't connect with their ex directly, they may look at old photos or reminisce, or even start an argument because even though it will be negative, they will both be battling the same conflict and feel connected.

There is so much more to say about the anxious attachment's relationship with breakups, but to keep on topic, we will move on. The most important thing to note here is that since the anxious doesn't have a relationship to self, if a breakup occurs, they will feel as though they have no identity, making the separation extremely painful.

A Secure Relationship

To become involved in a secure relationship, both you and your partner (whether current partner or future partner) will have to display traits of secure attachment. This means, already being secure, or intentionally working toward security if you have an insecure style. It is not ideal to become secure yourself and then find someone who isn't genuine about becoming secure and *fixing* them. For the relationship to be secure, it requires both partners working together.

We attract what we are. As you learn healthier ways to approach the world, other likeminded people will see that in you, and you will see it in them. When you change what's familiar to you and become aware of healthy patterns versus unhealthy patterns, you will become more attracted to security rather than old relationship patterns like the unavailable partner or the inconsistent partner or the partner whose love you have to earn or the partner that makes you prove yourself.

By knowing what you want in a relationship, you can find what you're looking for better. Even if you aren't actively searching, when a potential partner appears, you will be able to assess if they meet enough of your criteria for you to continue seeing them. And that's not to say they aren't good enough, but they just may not be the one for you. Remember to be living up to your own standards in the relationship to yourself.

As you work on topics we've discussed (we're about to open our toolkit in the next section), your self-esteem will grow, and you will feel surer of yourself, talk to yourself with compassion, and understand much of what others do is because of them. When you become a better person to yourself, you can become a better person to others and see better in others.

Toolkit

In this section, we will cover exercises you can do to promote a healthy dating experience having anxious attachment, focused on creating a secure attachment via secure thought processes and actions. We will break down tactics we've already discussed using forementioned tools and information from previous sections.

You can do these in any order and focus on the ones that help you with your struggles the most. Some of these will require revisitation daily for at least a month to get the full benefits as once they become habitual, you will begin doing them automatically, replacing unhealthy ways of thinking and coping mechanisms (protest behaviors) with healthy strategies.

The format of each tool will begin with the exercise followed by prompts within the exercise, including examples to guide you.

Amazing work putting in the effort! Keep it up.

Dating Stories

What stories do you bring into dating?

I will eventually be abandoned. There is no one out there for me.

_____

_____

_____

What is the cost in thinking this way about dating?

I hurt myself by thinking this way. I will settle.

_____

_____

_____

What are the benefits of being kinder in your way of thinking?

I empower myself. I feel better. I won't be as likely to settle.

_____

_____

_____

Can you reframe your dating stories?

It is normal to have dating experiences that don't work out. If it doesn't work out, it doesn't mean I will always be abandoned.

_____

_____

_____

Desired Traits in a Partner

What are traits you desire in a partner?

Understanding. Honesty. Caring. Humor. Chemistry. Confidence.

_____

_____

_____

_____

_____

_____

_____

_____

_____

Be aware that you have desirable traits, too. What are they?

Kindness. Humility. Humor. Caring. Honesty. Affection. Loving.

_____

_____

_____

_____

_____

_____

_____

_____

_____

(Non)-Negotiables

What are your preferences? (Things you'd be happy to see in a partner, but not required.)

Enjoying to cook. Having a similar music taste.

_____
_____
_____
_____

What are your standards? (Things you find important but that you can compromise while considering you both. Compromising the frequency or type you do together.)

Exploring the outdoors. Playing video games.

_____
_____
_____
_____

What are your non-negotiables? (Things that you require.)

Kids. Loyalty. Trustworthiness.

_____
_____
_____
_____

Relationship Fears

What are your fears in a relationship?

That my partner will grow tired of me. I'll be left.

_____

_____

_____

Are these fears realistic or something you've carried with you?

No, I've carried them with me.

_____

_____

_____

What can you replace these fears with?

Trusting what I have to offer. Understanding some relationships work out and some don't and it isn't a reflection on my worth.

_____

_____

_____

How can you do this?

Reminding myself of my positive traits. Building my self-esteem.

_____

_____

_____

Awareness

If helpful, skip to the exercises associated with each before filling this one out.

What are your core wounds?

_____

_____

_____

What are your needs?

_____

_____

_____

What are your boundaries?

_____

_____

_____

What are your triggers?

_____

_____

_____

What are your coping mechanisms/protest behaviors?

_____

_____

_____

Question Your Stories

Describe a situation you felt negatively about.

My date had to reschedule.

_____

_____

_____

What did you make this mean?

My date is getting second thoughts and doesn't want to see me.

_____

_____

_____

Do you know this with absolute certainty?

_____

What else could this mean?

My date could be nervous, too. An emergency could have happened. My date could have gotten called into work.

_____

_____

_____

_____

Identify Your Needs

What needs do you have? (For help, what needs are you drawn to? Think of someone you admire – what do you admire about them?)

I admire my friend who always gives time to listen to me. This friend encourages me and we do random fun things together.

_____

_____

_____

What needs can you find you have by looking at what you admire about this person?

Being heard. Understanding. Compassion. Encouragement. Spontaneity. Togetherness.

_____

_____

_____

Now with this in mind, what needs do you have?

_____

_____

_____

_____

_____

_____

Identify Your Needs Part II & Meet Your Own Needs

Think of a time you felt negatively.

My text went unanswered for hours.

_____

_____

_____

Which needs did you need fulfilled to feel relief?

Connection. Acknowledgment. Comfort. Certainty.

_____

_____

_____

How can you meet these needs yourself?

I can connect and acknowledge myself by spending quality time with myself journaling or reading or going for a walk. I can talk kindly to myself and take a warm bath for comfort. I can keep my promises to myself for certainty.

_____

_____

_____

_____

_____

_____

Dating Needs & Expressing Your Needs

What needs do you need in a relationship?

Certainty. Transparency. Connection. Consistency. Reassurance.

_____

_____

_____

Can you give these to yourself on some level? (Refer to the previous exercise for help.)

_____

_____

_____

Can you express these needs? Are there fears around doing this? Include why they are important and how they can be respected.

I have a need around transparency. It is important to me because without it, I can give situations a negative meaning. Can you use clear language with me so I can better understand?

_____

_____

_____

_____

_____

_____

_____

_____

Identify Your Boundaries

Think of a time you felt uncomfortable when someone did something.

My partner turned our date into a double date.

_____

_____

_____

How did you feel?

Blindsided. Anxious. Confused.

_____

_____

How was a boundary crossed?

I wasn't asked if I was comfortable with this and I wanted to connect one-on-one during this date.

_____

_____

_____

What did you need?

I needed to be a part of the decision, and in this case to have quality time.

_____

_____

_____

Respecting Boundaries

What is a boundary you have difficulty respecting?

My partner's space.

_____

_____

_____

What is your fear in respecting their boundary?

If I give them space, they'll forget me.

_____

_____

_____

What is a boundary of yours that you cross yourself?

Taking my coworkers shift when I can't.

_____

_____

_____

What fear do you have if you don't do this?

They will hold it against me and won't like me anymore.

_____

_____

_____

Question your stories here and consider yourself.

Expressing Your Boundaries

What was the boundary and how was it crossed?

When my partner made our date a double date without checking with me.

_____

_____

_____

Why is this boundary important to you?

I feel less anxious when I know what to expect, and I needed quality time with just my partner.

_____

_____

_____

How can you express this?

I understand you wanted us to spend time with friends, too, and I would love to sometime soon. However, a boundary was crossed for me when I wasn't included in the decision. I struggle with anxiety and when I know what to expect, I'm better able to prepare.

_____

_____

_____

_____

_____

_____

_____

_____

Identify Core Wounds

Think of a situation in which you felt negatively.

My partner was scrolling on the phone when we were spending time.

_____

_____

_____

How did you feel during this?

I felt hurt and bothered that my partner was giving more attention to the phone than to me.

_____

_____

_____

Look at the core wounds. Do any stick out to you during this situation and your thoughts and feelings associated with it?

I am rejected. I am unimportant. I am disconnected. I am not enough.

_____

_____

_____

_____

_____

_____

Healing Core Wounds

Which core wounds do you feel?

I am abandoned. I am unloved.

_____

_____

_____

Using the tool in the core wounds section, find their opposites.

I am connected. I am loved.

_____

_____

_____

Identify places in your life where you feel these positive ways.

I am connected to myself when I journal. My partner and I were connected when we had a heart-to-heart. I am loved by my dog. I am able to feel loved as I build my self-esteem.

_____

_____

_____

_____

_____

_____

_____

_____

Build Self-Esteem

How often do you speak negatively to yourself, and how would you benefit by speaking kindlier to yourself?

Countless times a day. I would empower myself and feel better.

_____

_____

_____

What is something you desire to accomplish but haven't yet?

I want to learn another language. I want to find a good partner.

_____

_____

_____

What reasons do you give for not accomplishing these yet?

I'm too stupid. I'll fail. No one wants me.

_____

_____

_____

How can you reframe these reasons? Create strategies.

It will take time, but with practice I can do it. I deserve a good partner.

_____

_____

_____

Building Self-Esteem Part II

How much do you compare yourself to others? Can you identify an example?

Often. My friend is okay with being alone and I'm not.

_____

_____

_____

What do you believe about yourself when you do this?

That I'm not good enough. That I'm weak.

_____

_____

_____

Is this comparison healthy? Does it make you feel good or bad?

I feel poorly about myself. It motivates me to give up rather than trying to be the best me I can be.

_____

_____

_____

Expectations

What is an expectation you had and you became disappointed?

My partner and I had off the same day so I expected we would spend the day together.

_____

_____

_____

What was your need behind this expectation?

I needed to feel connected. I needed to know that my partner wanted to spend the day off with me to feel important.

_____

_____

_____

Was this a fair expectation?

_____

How could you have gotten this need met?

I could have communicated with my partner that I would like to spend the day together if it suited us both, or found compromise together, perhaps finding a day that worked for us both. I could have connected with a friend, asked my partner for reassurance, created a strategy that would make myself feel important to me.

_____

_____

_____

_____

_____

_____

"Mind Reading" Expectation

When is a time you expected mind reading?

My birthday was approaching when I told my partner I really liked a shirt we saw in the store. I expected my partner to know I wanted it for my birthday.

_____

_____

_____

Was there a fear behind communicating this directly?

I didn't want to be a burden by asking for it and figured my partner would get the hint if they really listen to me.

_____

_____

_____

What did you make this fear mean about you?

That I'm not allowed to want things. That my partner doesn't care about me if they don't know what's on my mind.

_____

_____

_____

Can you reframe this?

By communicating, I can be heard and it lets my partner know what I need. It isn't fair to expect someone to read between the lines.

_____

_____

_____

Communicating Red Flags

What is a red flag you noticed with a date?

My date was rude to the cashier at the store.

_____
_____
_____

Is this non-negotiable or is it worth inquiring an explanation?

_____

Express this concern to your date. (If you feel comfortable and believe there is a connection.)

I noticed you said some potentially hurtful words to the cashier today. Kindness and respect are important to me, so it would help to know if there was a reason for this. (Of course there isn't an excuse to treat people poorly, but knowing whether, in this example, the date had a bad day and became easily irritable or if this is regular behavior for them can help you decide to continue or not.)

_____
_____
_____
_____
_____
_____
_____
_____
_____

Stop Abandoning Yourself

Where do you abandon yourself?

I cross my boundaries. I ignore my needs. I search for external company rather than getting to know myself.

_____

_____

_____

Why might you abandon yourself?

I think I'll be more liked always putting others ahead of myself. I don't trust myself to be alone.

_____

_____

_____

How is this harmful?

I don't respect myself. I grow resentful. My needs go unmet, causing discomfort. I constantly feel lonely without others.

_____

_____

_____

How can you be with yourself during these times?

I can respect my boundaries and needs. I can get to know myself by treating myself like a new friend and asking myself questions.

_____

_____

_____

People Pleasing

What are you afraid will happen if you don't people-please?

I'll be disliked and ultimately abandoned.

_____

_____

_____

Question this story. Then think of a time people pleasing has made you uncomfortable or resentful.

My date asked me to pay the whole dinner check even though we had agreed to split it this time, but I still paid it.

_____

_____

_____

How can you handle something like this next time?

I can remind my date that we agreed to split the check and respectfully make it clear that I only have enough money prepared to pay half.

_____

_____

_____

After your stories are questioned and you consider the fairness for all parties involved, minus the discomfort from the unfamiliarity, can you see how this is healthier?

_____

Drawing a Line Through Enmeshment

It is important to recognize that though a relationship requires connection, it is necessary for both partners to have their own space as well.

 Going back to this diagram, write what's *you*, *them*, and the two of you *together* in an ideal relationship.

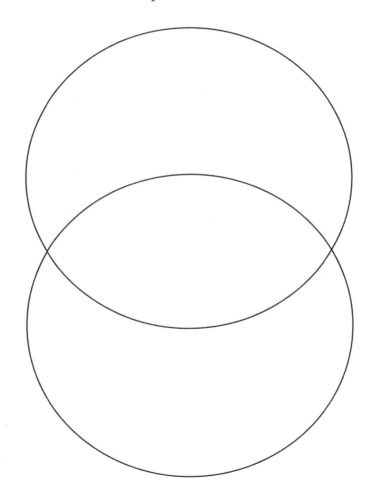

Replacing Protest Behaviors with Healthy Strategies

What is a coping mechanism/protest behavior you use?

Constantly texting.

_____

_____

_____

When do you use this protest behavior?

When I don't get a response or am being ignored.

_____

_____

_____

What need are you trying to meet by doing this?

Connection. Reassurance. Certainty.

_____

_____

_____

What is a healthier strategy to get these needs met?

*I can reassure myself by questioning my stories. I can communicate
to the other person my need for certainty while respecting their space.*

_____

_____

_____

Self-Soothing

How do you feel when a negative situation happens?

Anxious. Sad. Hurt. Worried. Scared.

_____

_____

_____

What do you need to feel better? What do you search for in others when you soothe through them?

Reassurance. Comfort. Understanding. Love. Care.

_____

_____

_____

Can you give these things to yourself? How?

Yes. I can question my stories. I can make myself tea and read a comforting book. I can go sit on the beach and speak kindly to myself.

_____

_____

_____

_____

_____

_____

This, like several of these exercises, won't come easy at first, but will be exceptionally worth it as they become familiar.

Abandonment

Think of a time when you felt abandoned.

When my partner broke up with me.

_____

_____

_____

Did you feel this was your fault?

Yes. My partner said I was too much.

_____

_____

_____

If you feel this way, how may it not have been your fault or not all your fault? Be compassionate.

We both had a role. My partner could have communicated.

_____

_____

_____

How has the fear of abandonment controlled your life?

I think less of myself and worry that if I mess up people will leave.

_____

_____

_____

Rejection

When you get rejected, real or perceived, what reasons do you give?

That I'm not good enough. That no one wants me.

_____

_____

_____

Do you know this is the reason? Then question your negative stories and work on self-esteem.

_____

_____

_____

How can you accept yourself?

By not speaking poorly to myself or jumping to negative conclusions I can't know are accurate. I can show myself compassion.

_____

_____

_____

_____

_____

_____

Anxiety Management

When you feel anxious, or other uncomfortable emotions, what do you do and think?

I get hot. I distrust myself to handle it.

_____

_____

_____

As this happens, where do you feel sensations in your body?

In my head and throat. My chest and stomach.

_____

_____

_____

What is this emotion trying to communicate?

I'm in danger. I'm scared or worried.

_____

_____

_____

What can you do to alleviate this?

Breathing techniques. Go for a walk. Create and give attention to positive thoughts.

_____

_____

_____

Perfect Dating Isn't Real

Is it fair to believe every date should be a success?

_____

When a date doesn't go well, what do you do or think?

I blame myself. I talk poorly to myself. I get worried. I get scared no dates will go well.

_____
_____
_____

What would you tell a friend whose date didn't go perfectly?

That not all dates are going to be great, but they'll get practice and find someone they connect with.

_____
_____
_____

Can you give yourself the same consideration? How can you encourage yourself after a date doesn't go perfectly?

_____
_____
_____
_____
_____
_____

Pretend Self

Do you notice yourself hiding your true self? What types of things do you do when this happens?

I fake my hobbies and interests to align with my partners. I hold back my opinions. I pretend to always want to do what they want to do.

_____

_____

_____

What are the negative effects of this?

I distance from myself and my own interests. I don't get to show them my world like they're showing me theirs. I grow resentful. I put on an act and it lowers my self-esteem.

_____

_____

_____

_____

What are your fears around why you do this?

I'm afraid I'll annoy them or they won't approve of me.

_____

_____

_____

If your true self distances someone, you'll have a chance to connect with someone else who really gets you for you.

Final Note

Healing core beliefs and correcting negative responses can be a difficult journey, but one extremely beneficial. It will take time and effort on your part. It will also be one of the most worthwhile things you do. Consistency is key with any type of success. By doing these exercises when a specific issue arises, or other worksheets you find helpful, will drastically improve your self-worth, your ability to communicate healthier, your self-talk, as well as time management and self-esteem and confidence. Don't worry if you have bad days, even while working on yourself. This isn't a heal-all. You're going to have good days and bad days, but I genuinely hope this workbook will help you have more good days and a better outlook on yourself and others.

Remember: Love isn't only something you get. It's also something you give.

Share Love ♥

Access the **free downloadable PDF**, *Attachment Breakthrough Guide and Worksheets Crash Course* by going to https://bit.ly/join-tgt or use your phone to scan the code below.

Take the **Attachment Quiz** by going to https://bit.ly/takequiztgt or use your phone to scan the code below.

Check out **more books** from The Growth Tutorial by going to https://amzn.to/3TFEstk or use your phone to scan the code below.

Made in the USA
Monee, IL
30 October 2024

68997151R00066